I'm Hungry!

YOUR GUIDE TO NUTRITIOUS
AND TASTY FOOD
FOR YOUNG CHILDREN

Eleanor Brownridge, R.P.Dt., F.C.D.A.
With recipes by Judi Kingry, P.H.Ec.

A Random House/Lorraine Greey Book

Canada's Food Guide is reproduced on page 204 with permission
of the Minister of Supply and Services Canada 1993.

Canadian Cataloguing in Publication Data

Brownridge, Eleanor
    I'm Hungry

ISBN 0-394-22347-0

1. Children — Nutrition.   I. Title.

RJ206.B76 1987   649'.3   C87-094281-6

Published by
Random House of Canada Limited
33 Yonge Street, Suite 210
Toronto, Ontario
M5E 1G4 Canada

Produced for Random House of Canada Limited by
Lorraine Greey Publications Limited
56 The Esplanade, Suite 303
Toronto, Ontario
M5E 1A7 Canada

Design by Fernley Hesse & Associates Ltd.

Printed in Canada

A Random House / Lorraine Greey Book

CONTENTS

of all your child eats throughout the day, and the week,
that determines the nutritional adequacy of his or her
diet.

ACKNOWLEDGEMENTS

While researching this book, I sought the advice of fellow dietitians and nutritionists across Canada. At this time I'd especially like to thank

- Judi Kingry, a creative home economist and mother, who developed all the wonderful, easy-to-prepare recipes in this book;
- Lorraine Greey, my mentor on this project, who read every draft, offered numerous useful suggestions and always maintained her enthusiasm;
- the late Jane Hope, my former partner, a dear friend and a loyal cheerleader, who constantly sent clippings and suggestions, and who carried a heavy share of our business while I was writing this book;
- Dr. Elizabeth Bright-See, chair of home economics at Brescia College, University of Western Ontario, for always knowing where to find the right information and for being ready to share her expertise;
- Sandra Matheson, dietitian and food management consultant, for providing many of the snack and lunch ideas;
- Pauline Flick, my assistant, who dared to critique each day's writing;

- Carolyn Clark, British Columbia dietitian, for making vegetarian cooking so easy and delicious;
- Susan Skoplianos, dietitian at University Hospital in London, Ontario, for sharing humorous experiences with her own children;
- Gayle Owen, nutritionist at the Kingston, Frontenac, Lennox and Addington Health Unit, for her experiences with many mothers;
- Nan Millette, out-patient dietitian at the Hospital for Sick Children in Toronto, for providing case studies as examples;
- the nutritionists at the Ontario Milk Marketing Board for their craft and daycare center ideas;
- and many other members of the Ontario and Canadian Dietetic Associations who shared their resource files, offered their support and recommended the first edition of this book to many parents.

I'd also like to thank Dr. Lance Levy for providing his unique expertise in the treatment of children with swallowing disorders. Dr. Levy has interviewed hundreds of children, some via the Bliss Board. They described some very frightening experiences they'd had while being fed by well-meaning adults and therapists.

Most importantly, I want to thank you, the readers. Your letters and comments have been very encouraging and helpful.

Last but not least, I'd like to thank my family — my husband, who has cheerfully supported all my ventures, and my children, who taught me more about family mealtimes than any scientific research studies. All three children are now adults who appreciate and enjoy healthy food, and they even thank me for steering them in the right direction.

Establishing healthy family eating habits sometimes seems difficult, but it is well worth the effort.

INTRODUCTION

This book has been written for all people interested in feeding young children. That includes parents, grandmothers, babysitters, neighbors, daycare and nursery school personnel — anyone who is a caregiver. However, for simplicity's sake, I've used the term *parents* throughout.

I have not written it for "Superparents," parents who are determined to do everything themselves. Rather, it will appeal to those who want to balance a busy personal and family schedule, with time to laugh and play.

If you like to cook — when you have time — I think you'll enjoy trying the many easy-to-use recipes in this book, developed by a creative home economist, food stylist and writer, Judi Kingry. Judi was responsible for developing most of the recipes and testing them with her own child.

But there are days better spent tobogganing with your children than cooking in the kitchen. That's why I have also included information on the myriad commercial foods that are readily available in the supermarket today. I've tried to separate out convenience foods that provide good food value from the costly, less nutritious options.

Working Parents Can Do It Right

A parent who works nine-to-five should feel confident that she can provide good nutrition for her family without overtaxing her time resources. A recent study of 2,000 households in the United States showed that children of working parents are not nutritionally deprived in comparison with children in families where the mother is a full-time homemaker.

The working moms served seven percent more salads and eight percent more eggs, while children in "traditional" homes consumed twenty-three percent more presweetened cereal, thirty-three percent more cookies, eleven percent more pizza and salty snacks, and twenty-five percent more candy.

How did the working mothers manage? It is to be hoped that children and husbands pitched in to help with the meal preparation. Good nutrition should be a family project. I hope the advice in this book helps you make healthy eating an enjoyable habit in your home.

1

THE FEEDING RELATIONSHIP

"I'm hungry" are words you can hear when a baby cries, when an infant crawls to the high chair, when a toddler shoves cereal into her mouth by the fistful, and when a preschooler asks for an apple.

Often such actions speak more clearly than words. The three-year-old who says, "I'm hungry," half-an-hour after lunch may be really saying, "I'm bored." The four-year-old who refuses to come to dinner may be just testing you. Will you let her watch TV instead?

As a parent, you can develop a sensitivity to your child's feeding cues. An infant is full when she spits out the nipple or turns her head away from the spoon. A toddler has had enough when she begins to play with her food, rather than eat it.

Complementary Rhythms

Mealtimes are easier when parents and child develop a complementary rhythm. I know that's sometimes impossible. The rhythm always seems to be changing. Just when you count on your toddler's being finished with a meal and ready to go out at three o'clock, she decides to change her nap routine. And

3

if you have more than one preschooler, don't expect them to have complementary routines. Chances are one will be a big breakfast eater, but the other will eat a better lunch.

That's parenting — flexibility and adaptability are needed if you want each child to develop at his or her own pace. In the long run, this is the less stressful option. You won't find yourself trapped in a battle of wills later on.

Taking the Lead

Responding to your child's cues doesn't mean giving up the parental responsibility to set limits.

Although demand feeding is generally desirable during infancy, the mother with a sleepy, underactive, breast-fed baby who is growing poorly may need to examine her milk supply or stroke the bottom of her baby's feet to keep her awake during a feeding.

During the toddler phase, part of learning involves testing limits. Be reasonable, but firm, about meal and snack time routine. Knowing what to expect gives your child a feeling of security so she can get on with the task of learning about herself.

Feeding young children isn't easy. The first time round, parents are usually very surprised at how much babies eat — and how little toddlers eat. Then there's the dawdling, the limited variety of foods, the food jags, the fickle nature of their likes and dislikes, and the extreme day-to-day ups and downs in appetite. It's easy for parents to become so concerned about the nutritional well-being of their offspring that they fail to notice what attitudes and eating habits they are fostering.

Therefore, before getting into the meat and potato topics of what foods to serve when, reflect on the feeding relationship between parents and their children. It can be a mirror of the overall parent-child relationship.

The mother who complains that her child won't eat unless forced to is revealing a great deal about her own need to dominate, and her child's need to defend herself against parental pressure.

When you offer food to young children, you're doing more than just providing nutrients for healthy physical growth and development. You're also creating opportunities for psychological and social growth.

With every meal and snack your child is

- establishing attitudes towards particular foods and the total eating experience;
- learning new developmental skills, such as drinking from a glass or handling a spoon — even how to flick peas from a fork;
- gaining important social skills around the give-and-take of the shared mealtime experience;
- realizing behavior expectations, such as sitting still and not throwing food;
- achieving independence — even when it means saying NO to squash.

It's natural that responsible parents who care about their child's health and want him to grow as an energetic child become concerned about every morsel he eats. Is he eating enough? Is he eating the right foods?

But when this concern overshadows the eating relationship, you may find yourself falling into the trap of urging your toddler to finish his cereal or at least take another two mouthfuls of peaches. Soon it becomes a game. "Find the bunny at the bottom of your dish." And when that no longer works, you progress to: "Finish your carrots so you can have dessert."

If your child is coaxed or bribed with food, even when he

is not hungry, he comes to associate mealtime not with plea-surable anticipation, but with anxiety. He isn't learning the meaning of hunger or satiety; he isn't learning to experience, interpret or trust his own reality.

Ideally, you would like your child to develop a positive attitude about himself and his world. To do that you must let him experience what it feels like when he's hungry, when he's full, and even the stomachache that follows overindulgence. If the parent takes over all decision making, the child does not gain self-awareness.

Ideally, the parent chooses the foods that are safe and appropriate, prepares them in ways that preserve their nutritional value and makes them appetizing, and serves meals with a smile at regular times. The child then decides how much, or whether to eat.

But What about Likes and Dislikes?

As parents, we believe it is part of our responsibility to en-courage our children to like a wide variety of foods. We are more likely to achieve this when we set good examples our-selves. You can hardly expect your child to be enthusiastic about spinach if Dad doesn't dig into greens.

But even when we are doing our best, children don't always follow suit. As one dietitian friend said, "My daughter loves all vegetables, but my son will eat only corn, lettuce and, under duress, three carrot coins."

Let's be realistic and honest. Most of us could name a number of foods we avoid eating. The only difference is, we rationalize our tastes — lamb is too fatty; orange juice too acidic; straw-berries tend to cause hives.

If we don't make issues out of our children's likes and dis-likes, chances are they'll soon change. One day a preschooler will tell you he doesn't like eggs; the next day he'll ask for a second serving of omelette. Preschoolers enticed with a reward to try a new food are less likely to go back to that food than those allowed to accept or reject it on their own. You'll find more advice in Chapter Seven on dealing with likes and dislikes. Suffice it to say at this point that issues such as forcing disliked food and restricting sweets shouldn't become so important that they take the fun out of eating. Consider the long term as well as the immediate consequences of eating, or not eating, a certain food.

Never Say Never

At the very start, let's explode the myth that you can be a perfect parent. You can't. And there's no sense setting yourself up to fail. You'll just feel guilty. After all, your children won't always like your cooking, and they won't always eat what you think is appropriate.

What you can be is a human parent, with the best intentions to feed your child healthy foods — most of the time, and to make eating a happy experience — most of the time. You'll be doing well if you strive for that standard and accept, with a laugh, the many times you don't achieve your goal.

One day, when my sister and I were both celebrating eight-months-down-and-only-one-more-to-go with a special lunch on the town, she gave me a piece of advice I've never forgotten: "When it comes to your children, *never say, I'll never*. You'll just end up eating your words."

Now, as a mother of three, I know that advice applies to feeding children and all other aspects of raising them.

When I read nutrition books and articles that advise caregivers to *never* bribe children with food, *never* treat desserts as more rewarding than vegetables, or *never* supplement with a bottle if you want to continue breast-feeding, I wonder if the authors have had children. Their advice may represent the ideal, but it's hard to always follow the ideal when you are raising one or more preschoolers.

Throughout this book, I've tried to blend pragmatism, not dogmatism, with nutrition fact. Options are offered as solutions to day-to-day feeding problems. You may choose one today, another tomorrow. Oh, I know consistency is important when raising children — but that's another ideal. If you choose the best option seventy-five percent of the time, you'll be doing very well.

By best option I mean the one that makes the most sense to you as the parent or caregiver for your child. In this book I provide nutrition facts, as understood and interpreted by professional dietitians and physicians in North America. But realize that nutrition information is coming from a growing body of scientific research. Interpretations change as we evaluate this new information.

In the past fifty years, we've seen the pendulum swing from breast-feeding to bottle-feeding and back to the breast. During my first pregnancy, I took iron supplements. Eighteen months later, when pregnant again, I found that iron plus folic acid supplements were in vogue.

Recently Dr. Benjamin Spock, the world's best-known baby doctor and author of *Baby and Child Care*, said that when he was born in 1903, doctors were advising mothers not to give babies solid food until they were a year old. By 1933, when he started his practice, doctors were saying five-month-old babies could handle solids. Later, it went down to one month. Now it's back to five months. "Each time we think: 'Now we have discovered the ultimate truth' — and we pass this on to patients," said Spock. "Then it turns out we've only discovered a piece of the truth."

Advice in books such as this one can be a guide. It can give you ideas as to what a two- or three-year-old child might enjoy. But books don't tell you as much as your own child can. Be confident in your own interpretation. The textbook advice may be to nurse for ten minutes on each side every four hours, but you may find your baby is content with a seven-minute nursing at three-hour intervals on one breast only. No doubt you'll be glad to hear that on this routine, some babies sleep up to ten hours straight at night.

2
BEGINNING WITH BABY
The First Four Months

In a 1975 article, Dr. Donald E. Hill, at that time a professor of pediatrics at the Hospital for Sick Children in Toronto, wrote: "During the past ten to fifteen years there has been a steady decline in the prevalence of breast-feeding and a simultaneous trend toward the early introduction of solid foods."

How quickly the pendulum swings. Ten years later, seventy-five percent of Canadian mothers are breast-feeding their babies — at least for the first few weeks — for the many good reasons listed in the table on page 15.

Probably the best reason to start nursing is that early breast-milk — called colostrum — contains compounds that provide some protection against intestinal infections and other diseases. It's been well documented that breast-fed infants have fewer intestinal illnesses in the crucial early months. Respiratory infections may also be reduced. Avoiding illness is very important, because in a tiny infant, fever, vomiting and diarrhea can be very serious. A baby doesn't have the reserves of fluids and energy that a larger person has.

Mothers who successfully nurse their babies find it to be an especially pleasurable and rewarding experience. The baby's sucking releases certain hormones in the mother which create

11

a feeling of well-being and relaxation. Some describe the feeling as akin to sexual stimulation.

Busy mothers often choose breast-feeding because it's easy to travel with their infants; they don't have to worry about carrying or refrigerating formula. Of course, it's harder to leave your infant behind when you're a nursing mom; you have to be sure your baby is ready to take a bottle of either your expressed breast-milk or formula from the substitute caregiver.

If members of your family have allergies to food or other compounds, your infant may be allergy-prone. By breast-feeding you may be able to delay problems until your baby is older and stronger.

But some of the traditional arguments used to encourage breast-feeding don't necessarily apply in Canada where the water supply is generally clean and safe, and refrigeration is available. Commercial infant formulas are safe to use if you follow the dilution directions carefully, prepare the formula in a clean environment and keep it refrigerated. Where water safety and refrigeration are problems, you can use ready-to-feed formula.

Commercial formulas are easy to use and closely mimic the nutritional composition of breast-milk (see page 30). There are many examples of healthy babies started exclusively on formula, indicating that the nutritional mix must have been close to ideal.

Some argue that formula preparation is time-consuming. That's true, but nursing mothers also need to budget plenty of time for adequate rest and breast care (see page 17). You can't expect your body to be able to do all the housework, care for other toddlers, attend numerous social functions, or hold down a demanding job at the same time it's manufacturing more than a litre of high-quality milk daily.

One argument often given against formula-feeding is that mothers who try to encourage their babies to finish the last ounce in the bottle may be overfeeding their babies, starting a habit that could lead to obesity later in life. But breast-fed babies can also be overfed. New mothers need to develop a sixth sense about their babies in order to distinguish between the need for extra sucking and cuddling, and hunger. Even when "feeding on demand," you don't need to offer the breast every time your baby fusses. If it isn't close to feeding time, try a hug, a rock, a change of position, a diaper change or even a pacifier instead.

My advice to expectant parents is to study carefully all the pros and cons of nursing and formula-feeding. Discuss your concerns with your mate and your doctor. I sincerely hope you'll decide to give breast-feeding a good try. But if after a few weeks you find it's not the right option for your family, you can switch to bottle-feeding without undue worries about your decision.

Breast-feeding

Exploding the Myths about Breast-feeding

- *Breast-feeding changes the shape of your breasts.* Your breasts won't sag later in life just because you nurse.
- *Nursing prevents pregnancy.* Breast-feeding is not a reliable contraceptive, although you may not have menstrual periods while nursing.
- *Once nursing has been well established, you can't miss any feedings without permanent damage to your milk supply.* Time away, even a week's vacation, is no reason to stop nursing. However, you'll need to express your milk twice a day while away, and it may take twenty-four hours for your milk supply to return to normal.
- *Every woman can breast-feed.* While the great majority of women can breast-feed — even with small breasts or multiple births — about ten percent can't because of breast

abnormalities, prolactin deficiencies, insufficient glandular tissue, etc. Heroic efforts are not necessary, nor are guilt feelings.

- *The more you breast-feed, the more milk you will make.* Infrequent nursing results in an insufficient milk supply. However, the converse is not true. An infant may be nursed at close intervals, yet obtain minimal milk volumes, either because the mother is too tired or too upset, or because she hasn't been drinking enough fluids. In the middle of a hot summer day, it's not uncommon for a mother's milk supply to dwindle unless she makes a great effort to take extra fluids. However, infrequent nursing can result in an insufficient milk supply, so make sure you don't supplement with too many bottles before your supply is firmly established.

- *Nursing prevents allergies.* Breast-feeding can delay the appearance of food allergy symptoms, and thus postpone the problems until the baby is older, but breast-feeding does not eliminate the problem. In fact, some infants are sensitive to certain proteins eaten by the mother, which then appear in her milk. Symptoms such as colic, vomiting, diarrhea, runny nose, bronchitis and rashes have been related to a sensitivity to foods in the mother's diet. In severe cases the nursing mother may have to limit her consumption of cow's milk, eggs, citrus fruits, chocolate or other foods.

Breast or Bottle:
Making the Choice

BREAST-FEEDING   BOTTLE-FEEDING

Advantages and disadvantages for the mother:

Breast-feeding provides time for special closeness with your baby — an emotionally enjoyable experience.

Bottle-feeding can also be a time of closeness — and an experience other family members can share.

If you choose to nurse in private, it can be a time for rest and revitalization.

You can bottle-feed anywhere.

During nursing you may experience firm contractions of the uterus which help reduce its size.

You are freer to attend exercise classes to get back in shape.

Calorie demands of nursing are equivalent to vigorous exercise, so you lose fat stores faster, even while eating generous meals.

You can start dieting right away.

Travel is easier with no concern about refrigerating formula.

It's easier to leave the baby with a sitter.

Nursing mothers must get adequate rest.

Your energy should return quickly after the baby is born.

BREAST-FEEDING	BOTTLE-FEEDING
You have to watch your diet, eat balanced meals and avoid certain foods that may upset your baby.	Your diet doesn't affect your baby — just you.
You need to avoid certain medications, limit your alcohol use and avoid smoking.	You don't need to worry about taking medications. However, all mothers need to be responsible in their use of alcohol. Avoid exposing your baby to second-hand smoke; it can be dangerous also.
At first, you may need to nurse every two to three hours.	Baby can usually wait four hours between feedings.
Breast-feeding can be uncomfortable, with engorged or leaking breasts and tender nipples.	You have to prepare formula daily; it takes time to warm a bottle — time that seems especially long in the middle of the night.

Advantages and disadvantages for baby:

Even very young babies react to the odor of their mother's breasts with an anticipation of a special kind of pleasure and cuddling.	Bottle-feeding is a time when either parent can be close to their baby.
Fewer gastrointestinal illnesses, because a compound in breast-milk, immune globulin (IgA) provides some protection against infection.	No similar compound in formula.

BREAST-FEEDING	BOTTLE-FEEDING
If mother has been exposed to polio virus and E. Coli infections, she passes along her antibodies.	No antibodies in formula.
Some allergy protection, although some babies are allergic even to foods the mother eats.	Baby may be allergic to formula, although alternatives are available.
Baby controls amount of food.	Mother is able to monitor food intake.
Quantity and composition of breast-milk changes as baby's needs change.	Can change formula if necessary.
Fat absorption better from breast-milk.	Modern formulas seem to be just as easily digested.

Costs:

Extra food for mother costs about $2.00 a day. Vitamin D supplement for infant costs 18 cents a day.	One day's formula costs $2.50 to $3.00 a day. No vitamin supplements needed.

Making Breast-feeding Easier

Although nursing is a normal physiologic activity, it does create demands upon our bodies. If you understand those demands, and make allowances for them, nursing usually proceeds well.

Preparation should start during pregnancy. Ask your physician to examine your breasts to be sure there are no potential physical difficulties. If you have an inverted nipple, your doctor can suggest exercises to reverse the condition.

Some experts advise preparing your nipples in the last trimester by daily exposure to air, application of lanolin cream, and gentle pulling and rolling between the thumb. Others believe this is not a good idea. Check with your doctor.

Before delivery, discuss with your doctor your desire for a minimum of anesthetic, so that your baby will be alert for an initial nursing soon after delivery. At this point nourishment is not the issue, however, the baby's sucking can stimulate your milk production.

Rooming-in makes it easier to nurse on demand, instead of by the hospital nursery schedule. During the first few days, the baby can be fed on demand every two to three hours. But, in a few weeks, you'll probably have a three-hour interval between daytime feedings.

Proper positioning of the baby on the breast makes it easier for your baby to "latch on" and can eliminate nipple soreness. You should be in a comfortable position, either sitting up in a chair with a pillow on your lap for baby, or propped up in bed. (Some mothers prefer to nurse lying down, but be careful, especially when you are tired, not to risk falling asleep on your baby.)

To nurse from the left breast, hold your baby in the crook of your left arm, with your hand under the baby's buttocks. Turn your baby so she faces you; your abdomens should be touching. After you've settled into the most comfortable position for you and baby, touch her right cheek (the one nearest your breast) with your nipple. Your baby has a rooting reflex. She will turn her lips towards an object that touches her mouth area and will open her mouth wide. Hold your left breast with four fingers below the nipple and the thumb above. Direct the whole nipple and part of the areola (the red area around the nipple) into the infant's open mouth.

Your baby's lips should curl out to cover much of the areola. If the way she has latched on doesn't feel very comfortable, try pulling down on her chin with your index finger. That will bring her lower lip out and allow her to pull more areola into her mouth. Even though your baby's nose is against your breast, she will be able to breath easily if properly positioned.

Newborns have a natural sucking reflex. The movement of your baby's tongue on the sinuses of the areola will stimulate the milk flow.

If your breasts are too engorged with milk for your baby to grasp, or if she doesn't start sucking, trying expressing a little of your milk into her mouth (see page 28).

The usual starting routine is about five minutes on each breast at each feeding. Gradually work up to ten minutes on the first breast and as long as baby wants on the second. Sucking is an important jaw exercise, so let your baby enjoy the experience as long as your nipples don't become sore. Alternate the starting breast. You can use a safety pin on your bra to remind you which breast was used last.

Before removing the baby from a breast, break the suction by putting a clean finger in the corner of the baby's mouth and pressing down on the breast.

When cleaning your nipples, avoid using soap or alcohol as they can cause dryness. If possible, air dry your nipples by leaving the bra flaps down between nursings. Alternatively use cloth — not paper or plastic — liners or pads in your bra, and change them whenever they become wet. If your nipples feel dry, use some of your own milk as a moisturizer.

If you do experience nipple soreness, try exposing them to dry heat — sunshine, a hair dryer on low, or even a sixty-watt light bulb a few inches away. Of course, be sensible and don't risk burning your breasts. If your breasts become hot, engorged, hard, reddish or very tender, see your doctor. Clogged milk ducts can become infected.

Going Solo

Many women who give breast-feeding a try, while in hospital, run into difficulties at home and give up too easily. The let-down reflex, which starts the milk flowing, is very dependent upon your moods. If you're nervous or upset — about your milk supply, other members of your family, whatever — some feedings may not proceed smoothly. And if that bothers you, the problem can quickly become worse. That's when you need some support from your mother, a friend who has breast-fed, your spouse, a public health nurse or your doctor. Don't be shy about discussing your problems. Find a buddy — someone who has been successful at breast-feeding, whom you can call when you have questions or need support. If you don't know anyone, contact the local chapter of the La Leche League. Frankly discuss your feelings about breast-feeding.

Sue was committed to breast-feeding. At the beginning it was easy. She and baby Tommy quickly fell into a routine of nursing every three hours during the day. And at night Tommy sometimes slept seven to nine hours at a stretch. Sue wasn't worried about her milk supply. Indeed some mornings she had an overabundance.

Sue's mother and husband had made it easy for her at the start. Grandmother took over all the meal preparation and kept the house in shape. Husband Bill was even willing to change diapers, on occasion. But after three weeks, Grandmother returned to her Winnipeg home. The following week Bill left on a delayed business trip for a couple of days. Sue decided this was a great time to entertain some of her colleagues from work. Tommy usually slept well between 7 and 10 P.M. But instead of enjoying an

*evening with her friends, Sue found herself jiggling a
fussy baby the entire time.*

Get as much rest as possible. That was Sue's problem. She had
plenty of milk when rested, but when she overdid it getting
ready for her friends, her milk supply dwindled. Even though
she tried to nurse in front of her friends, she wasn't comfortable and her let-down reflex did not work.

Not every cry is a demand to be fed; the baby may just be
uncomfortable and need to be burped, held, or have his position changed. Breast-fed babies generally don't swallow as
much air as bottle-fed babies, but both should be burped.

RELAX. Although society no longer frowns on breast-feeding
in public, many mothers find that nursing is more successful
when mom and babe are alone. Find a comfortable place to
nurse. If you have an older child, you may want a place where
he can snuggle up beside you with a picture book. Unhook
your telephone; turn on some soft music; and sometimes ask
a neighbor, spouse or student to amuse your toddler during
a feeding. This is especially important for that late afternoon
feed, when you may be tired. On occasion, a glass of wine or
beer will facilitate the let-down reflex, but regular alcohol
consumption is not a wise idea when nursing.

Mother's Diet when Nursing

If you're going to be feeding your baby from your own body
stores, you must eat the right foods.

---

*Kathy was a confident mother of three. She had nursed
all her children and found it worked well even when
travelling. When the youngest baby was two months
old, the family decided to take a short camping trip.
But when the weather reached the 30s one day,
everyone became irritable. The baby was extremely*

*fussy and wouldn't settle down, even when the family
sought refuge in an air-conditioned restaurant. Kathy
had nursed the baby just before dinner, but it wasn't
enough. However, a second nursing, immediately after
a hasty retreat from the restaurant worked. In
retrospect, Kathy realized the difficulty. She hadn't been
drinking nearly enough that day.*

Health and Welfare Canada recommends about 450 calories
per day more than a non-pregnant woman needs. For the
average-sized woman, that means about 2,550 to 2,950 calories a day, depending upon how active she is. Those extra
calories must also provide essential nutrients — extra protein,
vitamins and minerals.

A reasonable meal pattern for a nursing mother would include:

- Three to four servings of milk or milk products. One
  serving is 1 cup (250 mL) of milk, or 2 oz (50 g) of cheese,
  or ¾ cup (175 g) of yogurt.
- Six to eight servings of grain products. One serving is a
  slice of bread, or ¾ cup (175 mL) of cooked cereal, or 1
  oz (30 g) of ready-to-eat cereal. Count a bagel, or a bun,
  or 1 cup (250 mL) of pasta or rice as two servings.
- Six to eight servings of vegetables and fruit. One serving
  is a medium-sized piece of fruit, or ½ cup (125 mL) vegetables or juice, or 1 cup (250 mL) salad.
- Two or three servings of meat or alternatives. One serving is 2-3½ oz (50-100 g) meat, or 1-2 eggs, or ½-1 cup
  (125-250 mL) beans, or 2 tbsp (30 mL) peanut butter.

Milk — either skim, two percent or homogenized — is
especially important as a source of protein, calcium, vitamin
D, riboflavin and energy. One way to obtain the extra milk,

fluid or calories you need is to enjoy a Supershake while nursing, once or twice a day.

Supershake

½ cup	plain yogurt	125 mL
½ cup	raspberry or cranberry juice	125 mL
½	small banana, sliced	½
¼ cup	instant nonfat dry milk powder	50 mL
2 tbsp	frozen orange juice concentrate, thawed	25 mL
2 tbsp	wheat germ	25 mL

Combine yogurt, juice, banana, milk powder, concentrate and wheat germ in blender container. Purée. Serve immediately. (Keep this recipe handy; you can serve these Supershakes to your children when they're older.)
Yield: One 12-ounce (350-mL) serving.

If you can't drink milk because you're intolerant to the milk sugar lactose, if you or your baby are allergic to milk, or you just can't stand the taste, you'll need to include other sources of calcium, vitamin D and protein in your diet. You may be able to tolerate yogurt or cheese. As well, certain green vegetables contain calcium. If you're not using fluid milk or milk powder, take a vitamin D supplement daily.

While nursing, many women continue to take the same vitamin and mineral supplement they took during pregnancy, primarily for extra iron and vitamin B6.

Although you're probably anxious to get back to your pre-pregnancy weight, now is not the time to diet. Severe dieting can reduce your milk supply. If you continue to nurse, you'll probably return to your normal weight within three to six months, because producing a day's supply of milk requires 600 to 1,000 calories. Teenagers and underweight women should be especially careful not to diet while nursing; they don't have the nutritional reserves to spare.

What you eat can be transmitted in your milk to your baby. That includes strong-flavored foods and spices (such as cabbage, onions and garlic), certain drugs and medications, and certain proteins. Therefore, if your baby seems to be unusually fussy, think back over what you ate in the preceding twenty-four hours. Could it be that an unusual food or quantity of one food, eaten four to six hours earlier, is upsetting your baby?

Modest use of caffeine-containing beverages (coffee, tea, cocoa, cola and chocolate) doesn't seem to create problems — but too much can cause your baby to become irritable, hyperactive and wakeful.

Certain drugs should not be taken during breast-feeding because they appear in the breast-milk. Certain laxatives may cause your infant to have diarrhea. And even too much aspirin, transferred in breast-milk, can lead to intestinal bleeding. Be conservative and safe. Discuss all medications — both prescribed and over-the-counter — with your doctor before using. If you had been using the Pill, your doctor may recommend an alternative form of birth control, such as an IUD, condom, foam or diaphragm.

Alcohol does appear in breast-milk in approximately the same levels as in the mother's bloodstream. In excessive amounts, it inhibits the let-down reflex, depresses milk production, and may cause severe problems for the infant.

Let's hope you were able to give up smoking during your pregnancy. Now it's equally important to continue the no-smoking habit as nicotine is transferred in breast-milk. Heavy smoking, twenty to thirty cigarettes a day, can cause your infant to be nauseous and vomit. As well, regular smoking can decrease the volume of secreted milk. Even second-hand smoke will pollute your child's environment causing nicotine and its by-products to circulate in the baby's blood. It increases the risk of pneumonia and bronchitis. Never smoke while nursing or holding your baby.

PCB (polychlorinated biphenyl) pollution of breast-milk is one of the hot topics that surface every once in a while, scaring women away from breast-feeding. Although there is no documented proof of harmful levels of PCBs in mother's milk, you can reduce the risk by avoiding game fish that come from contaminated water: for example, cohoe salmon, eels, lake trout, catfish, smelts and sturgeon from the Great Lakes or Okanagan Valley. You can also reduce possible levels of PCBs in your milk by avoiding rapid weight loss — mobilizing fat stores releases PCBs into your blood and milk supply.

Is My Baby Getting Enough?

You can't see if your baby is getting enough breast-milk, but there are good signs:

- Eight feeds in twenty-four hours as a minimum at first.
- The baby often sleeps approximately two to three hours between feedings.
- You change six to eight wet diapers in twenty-four hours.
- Baby has frequent stools. A newborn's stool is yellowish-brown in color, semiliquid to soft, and has curds or a seed-like appearance. Some compare them to mustard, others to scrambled eggs. The color may change, depending upon what you eat. Fortunately, as long as your baby is solely on breast-milk, the odor is not strong. After a few months stools will become less frequent, maybe only once every two or three days. Actual constipation, with hard, dry stools, does not occur in healthy, exclusively breast-fed infants who are adequately nourished.
- Normal weight gain is about one ounce (twenty to thirty grams) per day at first.

- Your baby seems content, but cries and fusses at certain times of the day.

Your baby's weight gain is the most reliable way to assess the adequacy of your milk supply. But don't fall into the trap of weighing him before and after feeding, as that just causes anxiety. Instead, visit your doctor regularly so he can monitor weight gain and compare it to gains in height.

An average rate is

- two pounds (one kilogram) per month in the first three months;
- one pound (500 grams) per month in the next three months;
- half a pound (250 grams) per month in the next six months.

Expect growth spurts when your baby is about six weeks old, at three months, and again at six months. At these times your baby may need longer and more frequent feedings for a few days to stimulate an increase in your milk supply.

Be sure to talk with your doctor if:

- feedings are infrequent and generally brief.
- your infant wets only a few diapers each day, and the urine is strong in color and odor.
- stools are infrequent.
- your baby rarely cries, is lethargic, irritable or weakly responsive.
- weight gain is sporadic, or there is a weight loss.

Replacement Bottles

Most books warn you against supplementing with formula during the first four to six weeks because regular nursing can help to increase your milk supply. They also suggest that a baby can become nipple confused. But like many rules, this one can be broken. At times supplementing is the right answer.

If you're going to be returning to work soon or just want to leave your baby with a sitter while you go out, it's only fair to the caregiver to be sure your baby is accustomed to a bottle before you leave her.

Before I left hospital with my first baby, my pediatrician, Dr. William Hanley, gave me some advice which I've never forgotten: "Have your husband buy a small supply of formula before you go home. Then, if one feeding doesn't go right that first day, supplement. And no matter what, call me Monday morning, just to tell me how you're doing."

After all the welcoming home excitement, that first feeding wasn't adequate. I just couldn't relax in the new rocking chair, with in-laws partying below. So after nursing, I gave my baby a couple of ounces of formula. Then both of us slept for a couple of hours. The next nursing went smoothly; Kenny and I were back into a routine.

Over the weekend my husband and I saved up a million questions to ask Dr. Hanley. Of course by the time Monday morning rolled around, we'd figured out most of the answers on our own. But it was great to know he was there if we needed him.

If your baby has been successfully nursing for a few weeks, you may have difficulty, at first, convincing him to take a bottle from you. Already he knows and prefers the smell of your milk. Enlist the help of a spouse, friend or mother-in-law and leave the room. You can use recently boiled, cooled water, your own expressed milk, or formula for these supplementary bottles.

Expressing Milk

To express milk, first apply moist heat to your breasts — a warm facecloth, a hot shower or a bath — and massage gently. Place your thumb above and forefinger below the breast, behind the areola, then squeeze gently pressing back towards the chest. Avoid rubbing the nipple. Rotate your grasp around the breasts in order to empty all ducts. Express the milk into a sterile bottle, cover and cool immediately. Manual and electric pumps are available, and are useful if you will be expressing milk for a period of time (if, for example, your baby is in hospital) or if you have difficulty expressing milk manually.

Expressed breast-milk should not be kept in the refrigerator for more than twenty-four hours, as it has not been pasteurized. If you're trying to build up a supply of milk before returning to work, freeze your expressed milk at $-10°F$ ($-20°C$). You can add cooled milk to the container of already frozen milk, but keep track of the date the first milk was added. Breast-milk can be kept in the freezer compartment of a refrigerator for two weeks and up to six months in a chest freezer.

Before feeding, the frozen milk should be thawed slowly in a pan of warm water or under running cool water. Avoid excessive heat and don't use your microwave for thawing, as it will coagulate the protein and clog the nipple. Shake the milk gently just before feeding. If you are not using the milk immediately after thawing, be sure you store it in the refrigerator.

If your plan is to leave expressed milk with your caregiver when you return to work, start building up a supply several weeks in advance. While at work, express your milk and store it in the refrigerator.

If expressing doesn't work well for you, don't worry. Many babies adapt well to breast-milk morning and night, and formula at other times.

Nursing and Working

When you return to work the biggest challenge will be to get enough rest and to relax. For you, the ideal may be to return to work part-time at first, or to juggle your workday so that you have time to return home during your lunch break. You'll need more than one hour for a restful nursing.

Using Formula

Despite the advantages of nursing, there are many valid reasons why you may decide to use formula some or all of the time — the need to be separated from your baby because of illness (yours or his); the medications you are taking; an inadequate milk supply; lack of support from your other family members; time limitations because of your other obligations. Don't let over-enthusiastic proponents of breast-feeding make you feel guilty about your decision. Commercial infant formulas have high nutritional quality; babies thrive very well on them.

Mother's Comfort when Weaning

If you can wean your baby slowly, it will be easier on you. But sometimes babies must be weaned quickly. If you find your breasts are uncomfortably full, express a little milk. You may also find it helps to apply heat to your breasts by standing under a warm shower or taking a warm bath. In between, wear a snug-fitting bra. If necessary, your doctor can prescribe medication to ease your discomfort.

Formula, Not Cow's Milk, for Infants

You should not give unmodified cow's milk to a baby under nine months of age. Cow's milk has different proportions of protein, fat and carbohydrate than human milk. These may be right for a calf, but not for an infant. Infants don't digest cow's milk well; indeed, its protein may cause iron loss due to intestinal bleeding, and the solute load can lead to kidney problems.

Cow's Milk Is for Calves
— Human Milk for Babies

Comparison of Human Breast Milk, Cow's Milk and Infant Formula

	Human milk	Whole cow's milk	Infant formula (iron-fortified)
Energy (cal/1 L)	660-700	628	680
Caloric distribution			
% Protein	6 (mainly whey)	21 (mainly casein)	9 (whey or casein)
% Fat	53 (varies with mother's diet)	49 (butterfat)	48-50 (vegetable oils)
% Carbohydrates	41 (lactose)	30 (lactose)	41-43 (lactose and others)
Vitamin A (IU)	1898	1447	2500
Vitamin D (IU)	22	424	400
Vitamin C (mg)	43	8	55
Calcium (mg)	140	1224	400-500
Phosphorus (mg)	140	960	300-400
Iron (mg)	0.2	0.4	12-15

Both human milk and formulas have a lower percentage of protein than cow's milk. Protein is important for growth, but six to ten percent is plenty. Also the type of protein in breast-milk is predominantly whey, whereas in cow's milk the protein is mostly casein. Recent research also indicates that infants absorb minerals such as iron and zinc more easily from whey protein than from casein.

The percentage of calories from fat in breast-milk and formula is high (approximately 680 calories per litre). Infants need this concentrated source of calories. Without it, they just could not take in a sufficient volume of food to meet their energy needs.

Your mother or grandmother may have stories about how she made formula using evaporated milk, water and corn syrup. The recipe was designed to adjust the protein, fat and carbohydrate proportions in milk to suit an infant's needs. Evaporated milk was used because it is heat-treated, thus denaturing the protein. If cow's milk protein is not denatured, it can cause intestinal bleeding in young infants.

Grandmother's recipe worked, but now you have it easier. Infant-formula companies have carefully studied the composition of human milk and have devised products that copy this ideal standard. They've adjusted the proportions of the milk proteins — casein and whey — for easy absorption.

Cow's milk has a higher proportion of calcium to phosphorus than does breast-milk. Although adequate calcium is necessary for the infant's growing bones, research has shown that the proportion of calcium to phosphorus can be a factor in the absorption of calcium. That's why infant formulas are adjusted to provide approximately equal proportions of these nutrients.

The iron content of all milks is low. If the mother's diet was adequate during pregnancy, a full-term infant will be born with iron stores to last three to six months. Also, it's believed that the small amount of iron in human milk is in a form which can readily be used by the infant. Therefore the Canadian

Pediatric Society recommends full-term breast-fed babies be given iron-rich foods or an iron supplement by six months. Premature infants need iron sooner, by eight weeks of age.

Choosing the Right Formula

Infants who are not being breast-fed should be given iron-fortified formula until nine to twelve months of age. Before this age, regular cow's milk interferes with iron absorption and even causes iron losses. The resulting iron deficiency can have long-term devastating effects on brain development.

There are many formula options now available; ask your doctor which would be right for your baby. For example, there are special formulas for premature babies and for infants who require a higher energy intake because of low birth weight or illness. The soy-based formulas are for infants who have a problem digesting the milk sugar, lactose, or whose parents prefer a vegetarian product.

If there are allergies in your family, your doctor may recommend a special formula, such as Carnation "Good Start," in which the protein has been altered so that it is less likely to cause an allergic reaction. For babies who have already had a severe allergic reaction, other, more expensive, specialized formulas are used. There are also formulas for rare nutritional problems, such as phenylketonuria or PKU (see page 178).

Once your baby reaches six months of age and is beginning to eat other foods, ask your doctor about switching to a less expensive, iron-fortified formula, such as Carnation "Follow-Up," that has been specially designed to meet the nutritional needs of older babies.

Most formulas are available in three different forms:

- With ready-to-feed products you don't have to worry about mixing and dilution. Anytime you're unsure about the safety of the local water supply, or if refrigeration will be a problem while travelling, the extra expense for this formula is money well spent.

- Concentrated formulas are the most popular choice for routine use. They are more economical than ready-to-feed, and the daily preparation is relatively easy.
- Powders cost about the same as concentrated formula. Greater care is needed in dilution and mixing, but the smaller volume can save storage space.

When travelling, my emergency kit included bottles of sterilized water and a small container of measured powdered formula. If needed, I could add the powder to the water, and not even have to worry about heating the formula, as it was already at room temperature. It was such an economical alternative, that I didn't mind throwing out any leftover formula.

Formula Preparation

Warm milk is the ideal medium for bacteria growth. That's why you must take every precaution to reduce contamination. What would be a minor gastrointestinal infection in an adult can be very serious in an infant. Fever, vomiting and diarrhea are far more serious in a small baby who has fewer fluid and energy reserves.

Absolutely essential for a clean, safe formula are:

- effective cleaning equipment;
- a safe water supply (if there's any doubt, boil for five minutes);
- proper storage of formula;
- time to take care.

Whether using terminal heat sterilization or aseptic technique, you must start with clean bottles, nipples, caps and utensils. You'll find the bottles and nipples easier to clean if you rinse them in cold water immediately after using. For thorough cleaning of the inside of bottles, use soapy water and a bottle brush. Check that the nipple holes are not clogged by squeezing the water through the hole. Rinse with very hot water, and let bottles and nipples air dry on a rack, as dish towels carry germs. Also wash the tops of cans, the can opener and all utensils with warm soapy water before using. Disposable nursers eliminate the necessity of sterilizing the bottle, but you still have to boil the nipples and caps.

Aseptic Method of Sterilization

1. Place clean bottles, nipples, caps and necessary equipment (tongs, can opener, measuring cup, stirring spoon, etc.) in a large pot or kettle. Cover with water and boil for 5 minutes. (If the water in your dishwasher is at least 140°F (60°C), you can sterilize in it.)
2. Using tongs, remove the sterilized bottles and let them drain upside down on a clean towel.
3. In another kettle, boil the water to be used in the formula for 5 minutes, then allow it to cool to room temperature.
4. Before opening, shake the formula can well. If using concentrated liquid, or powder, measure the correct amount into the measuring cup and dilute according to the directions on the can. (For a simple one to one dilution of concentrate, you can add the correct proportions of formula and water directly to the bottles. Ready-to-feed formula can also be poured directly into the bottles.)
5. Fill the bottles with the amount of formula your baby will likely drink in one feeding — 3-6 oz (90-180 mL).
6. Use sterilized tongs to pick up the nipples and covers and put them on the bottles.
7. Store the prepared bottles in the refrigerator until feeding time.

Terminal Sterilization Method

1. Wash bottles, nipples, caps, can opener, tongs, measuring cup, stirring spoon and formula can top in hot soapy water. Rinse with very hot water and let air dry.
2. Measure the required amount of water into measuring cup and add concentrate or powder according to the package directions.
3. Pour the required amount of formula (the amount your baby will likely drink at one feeding) into the bottles, and cover each with nipple and cap. Don't tighten cap.
4. Place the bottles on a rack in a large kettle. Add about 3 in. (8 cm) of water to the kettle, cover and bring to a boil. Let boil for 25 minutes.
5. Remove the kettle from the heat and let cool to room temperature. Tighten the caps and refrigerate until feeding time. If you allow the bottles to cool slowly, there's less chance of a scum forming that can clog the nipples.

Additional Cautions

- Don't keep prepared formula in the refrigerator more than forty-eight hours. Ideally you should be making a fresh batch every twenty-four hours.
- After a feeding, throw out any leftover formula. Wasting a little milk is wiser than risking feeding your baby milk that could be contaminated with germs.
- Don't use a microwave oven to sterilize your formula. It doesn't work.

When Can You Stop Sterilizing?

There's probably little point in sterilizing bottles once your baby is crawling about and trying to put all manner of things

in his mouth. However, cleanliness and care in formula preparation is still essential because germs grow easily in milk.

Feeding with Formula

Generally babies prefer milk with at least the chill taken off.
Most parents warm the formula to body temperature, as in-
dicated by the wrist test. Place the bottle in a pot of warm
water or hold the bottle under the hot water tap. If using a
microwave oven to warm the formula before feedings, be sure
to shake the bottle after warming and test the temperature on
your wrist. During microwaving, hot spots can develop, and
the formula can quickly be overheated. Babies have been scalded
by formula heated in a microwave.

Hold and cuddle your baby in your arms, just as you would
to nurse. Tilt the bottle so the nipple is filled with milk. Put
the nipple in the baby's mouth, pressing it gently against the
inside of his lower lips and gums. If you let a little milk drip
into his mouth, his sucking reflex will take over. If the milk
doesn't seem to be coming out, it may be that the nipple is
clogged and you'll need a fresh clean nipple.

After a few minutes, remove the bottle and let him rest. You
can hold him over your shoulder and gently pat or rub his
back to see if he needs to burp. Then let him have the bottle
again.

Let your baby decide when he's finished; don't try to force
down a last ounce. You don't want to start a pattern of overeating. Sometimes he'll take more, sometimes less. That's normal.

A word of caution about bedtime bottles. Sucking can be
very restful, and often babies fall asleep during a feeding. While
this habit can make for easy bedtimes, it can be disastrous to
emerging teeth. Breast-milk and formula contain the sugar
lactose. And teeth bathed in this sugar, or the glucose in fruit
juices, are very prone to decay. "Nursing bottle syndrome" is
the term used by dentists to describe a sad situation of decayed

baby teeth at the front of the mouth. To avoid the problem, wipe your baby's gums and emerging teeth with a wet wash-cloth after every feeding, and don't leave a bottle in the crib with your baby. The baby who falls asleep with milk dripping into his mouth could end up choking.

I'm sure you've seen her. The eighteen-month-old miss walk-ing around the toy department with a bottle in her hand. She occasionally takes a swig, but is mostly using the bottle for comfort, rather than nourishment. Whenever I see such a baby I'm reminded of the drunkard who can't be separated from his bottle.

If you don't want your baby to develop this habit, restrict bottle use to times when she's sitting on your lap — even if she holds the bottle herself. Once you allow her to begin cruising with a bottle, you'll be into an argument situation. Instead, if she's energetic at mealtime, let her wander between feedings on your lap. She can come back to you for more milk, until you decide mealtime is over and put the bottle away.

Is this one of those "never say never" situations? Maybe. But there's a good reason for this advice: milk that is carried around for several hours is the ideal breeding ground for germs.

Other Beverages

Between feedings, you can always give your baby recently boiled, cooled water — without added sugar. It's one way of getting breast-fed babies accustomed to a nipple, although many breast-fed babies don't need the extra fluid.

At three to four months, if your baby seems to be hungry between meals, you can start offering juice. At this point you're doing several things: helping the breast-fed baby become ac-customed to a bottle; letting your baby experience new tastes; and offering a good source of vitamin C. Start with diluted, vitaminized apple juice — one teaspoon of juice to two tea-spoons of recently boiled, cooled water. Apple juice is a better choice than orange juice because it is less likely to cause an allergic reaction. Gradually increase the proportion of juice, until your baby is taking two to three ounces of pure juice by approximately four to five months of age.

You can use jars of commercial baby juices, or prepare your own. Strain fresh, unsweetened canned or frozen reconstituted juice through a fine mesh strainer to remove any pulp. Don't boil juice — heat will destroy the vitamin C content. Instead, to keep it as hygenic as possible, prepare a small amount at one time, and keep it covered in the refrigerator until use, separate from the family juice. Use juice within a day or two of preparation, as the vitamin C in juice is destroyed during exposure to heat, light or air.

Although fruit juice should be an important part of your baby's diet, some parents give too much. As a result their babies develop diarrhea. Limit juice to two 3-ounce (60-mL) servings a day.

Vitamin and Mineral Supplements for Babies

It used to be that all babies were routinely given a supplement of vitamins A, C and D, since that was all that was available. Now there are more choices for infant supplements and the recommendations have become more specific to complement the feeding regimen.

A vitamin D supplement (400 IU or 10 ug) should be given to all breast-fed babies, especially during the winter months. Vitamin D is sometimes called the sunshine vitamin. That's because when your skin is exposed to the ultraviolet rays of the sun, a compound in the skin is converted into vitamin D. If you have a summer baby, the chances of vitamin D deficiency are less, but I'd still recommend this supplement. Formula-fed babies don't need it because infant formulas and all commercially sold milk in Canada are fortified with vitamin D.

There's no need for vitamin A — the amounts in breast-milk, formula and cow's milk are adequate. Most babies are on fruit juices by four to six months, so will have an adequate intake of vitamin C.

Dietary iron deficiency is the most common nutritional problem in young children. In infants, it can result in delayed motor and brain development that persists years later. Since premature babies haven't had time to build up iron stores while in the womb, they need an iron supplement by eight weeks of age and for the entire first year. Be sure to administer the iron supplement carefully. Iron overdosing can be fatal.

Full-term infants who are exclusively breast-fed for the first six months absorb sufficient iron from their mother's milk to supplement their iron stores. But once they start eating other foods, iron absorption decreases. Therefore first foods should also contain iron. Iron-fortified infant cereals are a good choice.

Cow's milk is a poor source of iron, and in infants it can interfere with iron absorption from other sources. If not breast-feeding, use an iron-fortified formula until your baby is nine to twelve months of age.

If fluoride is available while the teeth are being formed beneath the gum line, the teeth formed will be harder and more resistant to decay. In many Canadian communities there is plenty of fluoride in the water supply, so supplements aren't necessary. However, if you live in a non-fluoridated area, check with your public health unit to determine whether your water has enough natural fluoride. (Between 0.3 and 1.0 ppm — parts per million — is considered ideal.) If your water has less than 0.3 ppm, begin fluoride supplements at about six months of age. Discuss the situation with your dentist before starting or discontinuing fluoride supplements.

If you are a nursing mother on a pure vegetarian diet and

not taking a vitamin B12 supplement, your milk may be deficient in this important nutrient. You should have your blood tested. The doctor may recommend a B12 supplement for the baby, at least until your baby is on formula or regular milk, eggs and meats. Read Chapter Twelve carefully before putting your baby on a vegetarian diet. Some vegetarian diets can be very dangerous, particularly for a small child.

3

WHEN MILK IS NO LONGER ENOUGH
Four to Nine Months

The other day I overheard a mother bragging, "They were both on Pablum at two weeks!" I wonder why the age of starting solids is used as a sign of advanced development? None of us likes to brag about how much weight we gained over Christmas!

Then I remembered the day my pediatrician told me my first-born was ready for cereals. That milestone was so important I stopped at the grocery store on the way home from the doctor's to buy the cereal. Afterwards I laughed at myself. As a dietitian working at Toronto's Hospital for Sick Children, I had been responsible for feeding decisions for many babies. But when it came to my own baby, the doctor's word was law. I hope that after reading this book, parents will have more confidence in their own decisions.

When to Start

There's little point in offering your baby solids until she's developmentally ready and actually needs the additional calories. Three to four months of age is soon enough; many nursing mothers prefer to wait up to six months so that their milk supply isn't jeopardized.

41

If you start too soon, you run into the problem of tongue protrusion. For the first four to five months, babies have a natural sucking reflex. When the nipple, or anything else, is put in their mouth, the tongue moves forward. This helps express milk from the nipple, but the tongue can get in the way when eating from a spoon. It prevents the transfer of solid food from the front of the mouth to the throat. Most of what you feed just drips back out.

If you wait a few months, this reflex action decreases. As well, your baby will be secreting more saliva, making the food easier to swallow. Besides, babies under a month old don't have the enzymes to fully digest cereals. Much of what goes into the tummy may come out the other end.

One of the reasons many parents want to start solids early is to encourage their baby to sleep through the night. Sometimes the two events do coincide, but information collected on many babies shows no correlation between the age at which solids are introduced and sleep pattern.

There are some very good reasons for waiting until your baby is ready. Milk is high in protein and calories. If you fill your child's stomach with cereals before she has the capacity to handle extra food, she will end up consuming fewer calories and less protein in a day.

In addition, with any new food you introduce, there is the risk of an allergic reaction — hives, rashes, stomach upset, gas pains, vomiting, diarrhea, even asthma. It's best if you can avoid such possibilities until your baby has gained more weight.

But don't wait too long before introducing solids. By six months, or sooner, babies need the extra energy cereals can provide. Also, they have to learn how to transfer food to the back of their mouths and how to swallow from a spoon. This is a critical developmental stage. If not encouraged to learn, babies will be lazy eaters.

The right time for starting solids varies from baby to baby. Your baby is ready for solids, when:

- She can sit up with support.
- She has control of her neck and head muscles; she can lean forward or turn away to give you cues to continue or to stop feeding.
- She is fussy and seems hungry two hours after her last feed, and water or juice no longer satisfy her. (Be sure it's not wet diapers that are disturbing your baby.)
- She is drinking more than thirty-two ounces (one litre) of milk in twenty-four hours.

Introducing Solids

When you are introducing solids, do it slowly, one food at a time, giving your baby time to experience the new tastes, textures and experiences without pressure. Probably much of the food will dribble back out, down her chin. This isn't a sign she's rejecting the food; it's just that she hasn't yet mastered the skill of using her tongue to transfer food to the back of her mouth. At this stage, learning to swallow is more important than calories.

When introducing solid foods:

- Begin the meal with the new food, unless baby is very hungry and fretting. In that case, take the edge off his hunger by nursing on one breast or giving some formula. After the solids, you can offer the second breast or the rest of the bottle.
- Start with small servings — one teaspoon once a day — and gradually work up to two to three tablespoons by the fifth day.
- Put a very small amount of food on the spoon, using a slim baby spoon, an egg spoon or a coffee spoon.

- Insert the spoon far enough into her mouth that she can suck from it.
- Offer new foods at lunchtime so that you can monitor your baby's response during the afternoon and evening, and hopefully avoid a sleepless night or a nasty rash.
- Introduce only one new food at a time. If, after a week of trial, that food has been accepted without allergic side effects you can go on to another food.
- If she seems to particularly dislike a certain food, don't force the issue. Otherwise you may be encouraging a habit of rejection. You can always try the food again another day, and if it is still unpopular, forget it for a month or so.
- If your baby starts coughing or sneezing after you've given her a mouthful, hold your hand or a washcloth an inch or so away from her mouth. That will save you from a shower of puréed peas.
- A baby's appetite varies from day to day, just as yours does. If you set goals for finishing so much food, you could be overfeeding your baby, and frustrating both of you.
- Expect to waste some food at this stage. Much of it will land on your baby's face, hands and bib. That's normal.
- Throw out leftover food from baby's dish. By now it could be contaminated with germs. If you keep the amount in the dish at a minimum, there will be less to discard after the meal. Besides, if you try to save leftovers from her dish for the next meal, you'll find that they've turned to liquid. When some of your baby's saliva becomes mixed with the food, the enzymes in it break down the food's starch, the substance that gives the food much of its structure.
- Most important, serve with a smile; your mood will be catching.

Mealtime as a Happy Time

Although nutrition is a serious subject, that's no reason for making mealtimes somber. Go ahead and sing, make faces, and laugh during meals. Let your baby play with a toy while you're feeding him. However, try to avoid falling into the trap of using games like "Open wide. Here comes the airplane" to force feed. There's a limit to the amount of calories and nutrients your baby needs each day, and his normal appetite will determine this. Charts on menus and serving sizes are guides, but your baby doesn't need to follow them. And don't be concerned if your baby gives up eating completely for a day or so. Milk will do just fine that day.

Start with Cereal

Infant cereals are usually the first solid because they are an important source of iron, a necessary additional nutrient at this time of life to build healthy red blood cells.

All infant cereals in Canada are fortified with a form of iron that is readily used by infants. Six tablespoons of infant cereal provide the day's iron requirement. If your formula-fed baby isn't taking infant cereal by four months (six months if breast-fed), use an iron supplement or a formula that has added iron.

Rice cereal, not mixed with any other grain, fruit or vegetable, is a good first choice as it's the least likely to stimulate allergic reactions. After your baby has become well established on rice cereal for a week or more, you can vary the diet by trying other single grain cereals such as oatmeal and barley — one at a time. You'll want to avoid mixed cereals and cereals with fruit until each of the ingredients has been tried alone.

When you first use infant cereals, mix three parts breast-milk, formula or sterile water with one part infant cereal. Later, as your baby becomes accustomed to swallowing, you can increase the proportion of cereal.

You'll see by the label that some brands of infant cereals contain about forty percent infant formula. These are especially convenient for the nursing mother, as you just need to add recently boiled, cooled water. Don't add milk or formula to these cereals or they will be too concentrated.

Don't add any sugar, honey or other sweetener. Your baby doesn't need them. For the same reason, most nutritionists recommend infant cereals without added sugar. We're trying to discourage an early sweet tooth. (See page 65 concerning botulism danger from honey.)

Finally, don't be in a hurry to switch your baby from infant cereals to adult-type cereals. The texture of infant cereals is perfect for a young baby, and the iron content is right for up to two years. Other cereals, hot or cold, have only one-third to one-half as much iron, and the form of iron in these cereals is not absorbed as well by infants. Also, many adult-type cereals have far more salt and sugar than babies need.

Vegetables and Fruits

Once cereals are well received, you can move on to introducing vegetables and fruits. These foods are excellent sources of vitamins A and C, as well as several B vitamins and essential minerals. Most nutritionists recommend vegetables before fruits, believing that once your baby gets used to the sweeter taste, it's harder to encourage her to accept vegetables. Don't add salt, sugar, butter or margarine.

Commercially prepared strained carrots or squash are good first choices. Vegetables with skins, such as peas or corn, should be given last as they are harder to digest and may produce gas. Continue to stick to the *one new food at a time* sequence so you can determine any food intolerances or allergies. After at least four to five days on a new vegetable, you can try another, say green or yellow beans or sweet potatoes. Delay using vegetable or fruit combinations until your baby has tried each individual food alone.

Fruits such as puréed applesauce, apricots, peaches, pears, prunes and ripe bananas are favorite choices. Fruit and fruit juices are helpful if you've been feeding your baby too much rice cereal and she's become constipated.

Caution: Carrots, beets and spinach contain a compound called nitrate. During storage this nitrate can change to nitrite, a compound that can be harmful to young infants. The nitrite oxidizes the iron in the baby's hemoglobin resulting in the formation of methemoglobin. When this happens, the blood cannot carry as much oxygen.

To avoid this problem, don't serve home-prepared carrots, beets and spinach to babies under six months of age. For older babies, you can serve a fresh purée of these vegetables, but do not store or freeze quantities of them. Commercial baby food with vegetables does not have this problem because the storage time between picking and processing is greatly reduced, and the sterile environment reduces the risk of nitrite formation.

Meats Are Next

Start with strained chicken, turkey or lamb, as they are least likely to cause allergy problems. After these meats have been well accepted, you can introduce beef, veal, pork and liver. If you're making your own baby food (see page 52), you can also introduce fish, but be sure to remove all skin, bones and scales. Cooked legumes (peas and beans) and tofu are alternative protein sources that are easy to purée yourself.

A cooked egg yolk finely mashed can be tried about one month after meats. However, delay whole eggs, or egg white, until your baby is at least twelve months old; egg white often causes allergy problems.

Dessert

Desserts of puddings and custards aren't necessary, but they do add variety to your baby's menus. They are additions to use, on occasion, when your baby is particularly hungry. These products should not take the place of fruit or milk. The commercial infant desserts are low in sugar. If you're making your own, use half the usual amount of sugar in your recipes.

Yogurt also makes a good dessert. For babies, use plain yogurt rather than the fruit-flavored products; it has less sugar. You can add a little of baby's own strained fruit, if you like, to flavor the yogurt.

Foods in the First Year

Birth to 3 months	• 6-8 feedings of breast-milk or infant formula (20-32 oz/600-1,000 mL per day)
3 to 6 months	• 4-5 feedings of breast-milk or formula (up to 40 oz/1.2 L per day) • introduce iron-enriched infant cereal • start with 1 tsp/5 mL of a single-grain cereal — rice, oats or barley • gradually work up to approximately 6 tbsp/75 mL a day • delay wheat, soya and mixed cereals until later • diluted apple juice (up to 4 oz/125 mL per day)
5 to 7 months	• 4-5 feedings of breast-milk or formula (up to 40 oz/1.2 L per day) • cereals of all varieties, but without added sugar (up to 8 tbsp/100 mL per day) • cereal can be offered at breakfast and dinner

- strained vegetables, then fruits, one at a time (gradually work up to 6-8 tbsp/75-100 mL a day)
- diluted apple juice (4 oz/125 mL per day)

7 to 9 months

- 3-4 feedings of breast-milk or formula (24-32 oz/600-1,000 mL per day)
- may start cup
- continue to use iron-fortified infant cereals (up to 8 tbsp/100 mL per day)
- strained and mashed vegetables (up to 4 tbsp/50 mL per day)
- try mashed potatoes (no salt) and fruits such as mashed banana
- start to introduce puréed meats — chicken, turkey and lamb first (1-4 tsp/5-20 mL)
- puréed legumes — peas, beans and lentils (1-4 tsp/5-20mL)
- yogurt, cottage cheese and yogurt (1-4 tsp/5-20 mL)
- if no allergies, try orange juice (up to 4 oz/125 mL)
- dried bread products (whole wheat or enriched)

10 months on

- 3 feedings of breast-milk, formula or whole milk (up to 24 oz/750 mL)
- gradually introduce table foods
- egg yolks (start slowly, work up to maximum of 2 per day)
- puddings & custards (2-4 tbsp/25-50 mL) — keep added sugar to a minimum

Baby is now making a transition to family foods. See Chapter Five.

Note: All formula should be iron-fortified.

Homemade or Commercial Baby Food

You'll want to consider the option of making your own baby food versus buying commercial foods. The choice depends more on your time and inclination than on nutritional factors. The cost advantage of making your own baby food varies according to the season of the year. Many parents use a combination of homemade and commercial foods, secure in the knowledge that both options can provide the baby with nourishing, tasty foods, and a good introduction to family eating.

Many arguments against using commercial baby foods — such as too many additives, and too much sugar and salt — are no longer valid. Below are the facts.

The Canadian Food and Drugs Act and Regulations controls the use of additives in baby foods, as follows:

- Ascorbic acid (vitamin C) is allowed in dry cereals containing banana to keep the banana from discoloring.
- Soyabean lecithin (a natural food product) is allowed in rice cereals to prevent sticking in the manufacturing process and to enhance the flavor.
- Citric acid (a compound found in fruit juices) may be used to shorten the heating process, thereby helping to maintain product color and flavor.
- Monosodium glutamate, a flavor enhancer that came under much criticism several years ago, was withdrawn from all Canadian baby foods in 1969.
- Sodium chloride (table salt) is not allowed in strained fruit, fruit juice, fruit drink or cereals. Low maximum levels have been established for strained desserts, junior meat, meat dinners, dinners and breakfasts (often less than in homemade varieties). Since 1976, two Canadian baby food manufacturers have eliminated all added salt from their products. The label will tell you whether salt has been added or not.

- Hydrolyzed vegetable protein, also a source of sodium, has been removed from baby foods.
- Baby food manufacturers have greatly reduced the amount of sugar added to baby foods. The present maximum is nine percent by weight (down from sixteen percent), but many foods have no sugar, or at the most four to five percent. From the ingredient label, you can tell whether any sugar has been added as all ingredients must be listed in order by weight.
- Modified starches, from natural products such as wheat, oat, rice and potato flours, are added to baby foods to maintain the solid or semisolid consistency of these foods. Otherwise they'd be too liquid to serve easily from a spoon. These starches are a source of energy for infants; they're not harmful.
- Water is a necessary addition for some of the meats in order to attain the smooth consistency necessary for an infant food. The amount manufacturers add is similar to the amount you'd need to make a smooth purée.

The Baby Food Choices

Commercial Baby Food	Homemade Baby Food
No preparation time.	With food mill or blender preparation is relatively easy (especially fruits and vegetables).
Easy to use and store.	Must be stored in refrigerator or freezer.
Easy to carry with you and serve anywhere, especially the instant kind.	Baby eats same food as family.

Commercial Baby Food	Homemade Baby Food
Wide variety in all seasons.	Can try vegetables such as broccoli, cauliflower and asparagus that are not available in commercial baby food.
Manufacturers start with natural and fresh ingredients.	Can use natural and fresh ingredients in season.
Not dependent on family eating habits or times.	With prefrozen homemade baby foods you are also not tied into family food choices.
Controlled consistency and nutritional value.	Nutritional quality is up to you. It depends upon the ingredients you use and the careful way you prepare the food.
Guaranteed sterile.	You must prepare under sterile conditions.
Least expensive way to serve out-of-season foods.	Less expensive for foods that are in season, or foods your family will be eating anyway.

Making Your Own Baby Food

The above arguments are not designed to discourage you from making your own baby food. With a food mill, blender or a sieve, it's relatively easy. Homemade baby food is most economical when you can use foods your family will be eating at the next meal, or if you prepare and freeze batches of seasonal produce. You won't be saving money if you buy already-processed foods, or imported out-of-season produce to turn into baby food.

Your homemade baby food is only as safe and nutritious as you make it. Therefore follow these precautions:

- Start with fresh or frozen produce and lean meats. During storage, unprocessed fruits and vegetables lose nutrients. It's fine to use frozen produce and meats providing no salt has been added. However, you won't be saving money if you use canned products. In any case, canned fruits usually have added sugar, and canned vegetables often have added salt — unnecessary and possibly harmful additions for baby. Also, avoid cured meats, such as ham; they are too high in sodium (salt) for babies.
- Cook your foods in minimum water. Use all the cooking water for blending as it will contain many of the vitamins. Steam or microwave cooking are useful ways to cook with minimum added water. But use a low heat (or LOW microwave power) to keep meat tender.
- Keep your recipes simple. Babies don't need added salt, sugar, honey, molasses or other sweetener, butter or margarine, spices or herbs.
- Be sure your hands and all your utensils are clean. Wash knives, spoons, bowls, blenders and cutting boards in hot, soapy water just before using; rinse in boiling water, and let air dry.
- Work quickly so that food is not left for long periods at room temperature to allow bacterial growth. Besides, if you purée the food while it's hot, it's easier to get a smooth mixture. Even a small lump can cause an infant to choke.
- If you are using a blender or food processor, it's best to start with an ON/OFF pulsing action until all the food is finely chopped. Then use a continuous action until puréed.
- Unless your baby is eating the purée right away, refrigerate or freeze it as soon as it has cooled to room temperature.
- Use refrigerated purée within two days; freeze the rest.

- The easiest way to store serving-size portions for your infant is to pour two to three teaspoons of your blended mixtures into ice cube trays. Cover the trays with waxed paper, and freeze quickly in the coldest part of your freezer. Alternatively you can freeze lumps of puréed food on waxed paper placed on a cookie sheet or plate. Once frozen, store the individual cubes in tightly sealed freezer bags (one bag per kind of food) in the coldest part of the freezer. Label with date and ingredient.
- Frozen cubes should not be kept more than two months in a refrigerator freezer, or four months in a chest-type freezer.
- Individual servings are easy to thaw in a custard cup set in a pan of hot water, or in an egg poacher. A microwave oven is also useful for instant thawing and warming, but read the cautions on page 59 first.
- Use thawed cubes immediately. Do not refreeze.
- If you're going out for the afternoon, place a frozen cube or two in a small jar or plastic container and cover. By mealtime it will be thawed, ready for warming and serving.
- Your homemade purées may be more concentrated than the commercial baby food, so your baby may eat less in a serving. Alternatively, you can dilute your purées with some baby cereal.

Recipes for Homemade Baby Food

Puréed Fruits

| 1 cup | ripe fruit* | 250 mL |
| ¼ cup | water or fruit juice | 75 mL |

Wash, peel and cut the fruit into small pieces. In a covered saucepan, simmer fruit in water over low heat for 5-10 minutes or until tender. (In a microwave oven, simmer until soft, less than 5 minutes.)

In a blender or food processor, process fruit and cooking water using an ON/OFF pulsing action for 15-30 seconds. To test for smoothness, remove a small amount and rub between your fingers. It should be silky smooth.

If the fruit is stringy and your baby is very young, be sure to sieve after stewing. If you don't have a blender, mash cooked fruit with a fork or in a food mill and pass through a fine sieve.

Either serve immediately when cooled or refrigerate servings to be used in the next 48 hours. Freeze remainder.
Yield: about 1 cup (250 mL) or 4-6 servings.

*Apples, peaches, pears, plums or apricots

Puréed Soft Fruits

Ripe bananas, persimmons and kiwi fruit are easy to mash for babies — with a little fruit juice, if necessary. If your baby is very young, pass the mashed fruit through a sieve before serving.

Since your baby will eat only a small portion of a banana, peel and wrap banana chunks and store in the freezer. The chunks are easy to mash and serve after thawing.

Puréed Vegetables

| 1 cup | vegetables* | 250 mL |
| ¼ cup or less | water | 75 mL or less |

Peel, if necessary, and slice fresh or frozen vegetables. Simmer vegetables, covered, in a minimum amount of water until tender. If you are using a microwave oven, cook on HIGH (100% power) until just tender.

In a blender or food processor, process vegetable and cooking water using an ON/OFF pulsing action for 1-2 minutes to make a smooth purée. For very young babies, or when the vegetable

is stringy, force the purée through a sieve. If you don't have a blender, mash cooked vegetable with a fork or in a food mill and pass through a fine sieve. Use or store as for fruit.
Yield: about 1 cup (250 mL) or 4-6 servings.

*Sweet potatoes, peas, green beans or squash

Once baby is chewing, at eight or nine months, you can serve mashed vegetables, such as potato, or rice. Even at this age, your child doesn't need any butter, margarine or salt. Add a bit of milk to moisten mashed potatoes. Rice could be cooked in juice rather than water for extra flavor.

Puréed Meats

| ¾ cup | finely cubed lean meat (not ground meat) | 175 mL |
| ⅓ cup | liquid (water, vegetable broth, without salt) | 75 mL |

Meats are the hardest foods to make into a homemade purée smooth enough for a young baby. Generally you can't use homemade meats until the baby is ready to eat food with a coarser texture.

Start with very lean meat, remove all the gristle and cut the meat into small chunks. Since you will be using all the meat juices in the purée, it's not necessary to brown the meat first. Add the liquid and stew over low heat until tender. (If you cook in a pressure cooker, the meat will be very tender. You can microwave the meat at MEDIUM (50%) — no higher or it will toughen.) After cooking, skim off all the surface fat. In a blender or food processor, using an ON/OFF pulsing action, purée until all the meat has been finely chopped. Alternatively, you can use a food mill.

For a smoother meat mixture, add a small amount of rice cereal, formula or milk.

Baby's Stew

Once your baby is eating a wide variety of foods individually, you can make simple stew combinations of cooked meats and vegetables (for example, Gonzo's Chicken Soup on page 159). Just take out baby's portion before adding the spices, salt and sauces the family likes, and purée as for meats.

Puréed Fish

Start with boneless white fish such as haddock, sole, Boston bluefish or perch. Poach in milk and purée as for meats.

Egg Yolk

Egg yolk, separated from the white, can be poached conventionally in hot water, an egg poacher or microwave oven. Alternatively, hard-cook an egg, then separate the yolk, and mash it with a little milk. (Babies shouldn't be given egg white until they are twelve months of age because of the risk of allergic reactions. Eat the white yourself. It's a good source of protein, without fat.)

Tofu

Although tofu has been a staple of the Oriental diet for more than 2,000 years, Canadian parents are just discovering this white, custardy soybean cake. Tofu has many advantages as a baby food — smooth consistency, low cost, high protein, extreme versatility and easy digestibility. Tofu is high in protein and iron. Certain, but not all, types are also a good source of calcium. (It depends on whether the manufacturer uses calcium chloride or magnesium chloride to curdle the soy milk.)

There are two common forms of tofu — the regular soy milk or Chinese style, which is sometimes labelled soft because it is easily crumbled and blended into puddings, and the firmer Korean or Japanese style suitable for slicing and cubing.

For young babies the softer tofu is easier to prepare and contains more calcium. Drain water from the portion of tofu to be used. If the tofu is still runny, place it in a clean cloth, twist the cloth closed and squeeze or knead the tofu for 2-3 minutes, being careful not to press so hard that the tofu begins to come through. Mash and serve as is, or mix with pureed fruit or vegetables.

Tofu Yogurt

4 oz	tofu (water packed), drained and cut into cubes	100 g
⅓ cup	milk	75 mL
2 tbsp	frozen orange juice concentrate	25 mL

In a blender or food processor, combine tofu, milk and juice concentrate. Purée until smooth. Serve immediately or chill. You can add a topping of baby's favorite puréed fruit.
Yield: about 1 cup (250 mL).

Buying Commercial Baby Food

If you read the ingredient labels, you can easily determine what is in the food you are selecting for your baby. All ingredients must be listed on the label in order by weight. Although you may enjoy trying combination dishes yourself, your baby doesn't tire of plain fruits, vegetables and meats. Therefore stick to the simple foods most of the time; allow your baby to experience and appreciate individual flavors.

Probably the only time you'll need the combination dinners is when you're travelling with your baby and want to carry a minimum number of jars. There are three kinds of dinners. Meat-vegetable dinners, which list beef or another meat as the first ingredient, must contain at least twenty-five percent meat and are therefore appropriate for main meals. In vegetable-meat combinations or pasta-meat combinations, the amount of meat is considerably less. However, these are appropriate for smaller meals.

Commercial baby foods can be stored unopened or sealed for a long time (up to one year for strained juices and cereals, two to three years for fruits, vegetables and meats in jars). When you are opening a jar of baby food, listen for the familiar "pfftpopp" sound, proof that the vacuum seal has not been broken. Don't use a jar with a lid that is raised or bulging, or if the seal has been broken.

Once opened, unused portions of commercial baby food can be kept covered in the refrigerator for up to three days. Unless your baby can eat a full jar at one meal, don't feed him directly from the jar. His saliva will be transferred to the contents from the spoon. And the enzymes in the saliva can cause any food left in the jar to break down to a watery consistency.

If you're not in the habit of reading package labels, start now. You need to know what your baby is eating. Ingredients are listed in order by weight, from most to least. If sugar, for example, is near the beginning, it may be present in excessive amounts, but if listed at the end, a smaller amount has been added.

Microwaving Baby Food

Microwave ovens are great timesavers for busy families. And if you are using one for much of your cooking, no doubt you'll be anxious to use it for baby food as well.

But first, a few words of caution.

- After microwaving anything, stir or shake it, then test all food and formula before giving it to your baby. When you microwave food, it can develop scalding hot spots even when the surface, bottle or dish feels cool to the touch.

Allow the food to stand for a few minutes after it comes out of the microwave so the heat can dissipate evenly throughout, then test for temperature.

- Warm, don't overheat or cook the food. Babies like their food warm, not hot. A few drops of formula or food on your wrist should tell you if the food is about body temperature.

- Adjust the warming time to the amount of food. It takes considerably less time to warm a few ounces of milk or food than a full bottle or bowl. Babies have been scalded when sitters reheated a partial bottle in the microwave for the same length of time as a full bottle. To be safe, don't allow sitters to use the microwave oven for heating your baby's food. A pan of hot water is usually adequate and much safer.

- Nursers with disposable liners cannot be put in the microwave as they may overheat and break. Remove the nipple before putting a bottle in the microwave or it will age more quickly, becoming gummy in one to two weeks, rather than in two to three months.

- Don't microwave commercial baby meats or dinners in the jar. The droplets of water in these products heat faster than the protein and fat particles. Pockets of steam can form, leading to hot spatters — even a broken jar. It's better to transfer the amount of food the baby will eat from the jar to a shallow microwave-safe bowl; then heat on low to medium setting for less than forty-five seconds. (Note: The time depends upon the amount of food; half a jar takes less than twenty-five seconds.)

Ready for Teething Foods

Sometime between six to nine months of age, you'll notice your baby's gums are hardening, and the first baby teeth may even appear. This is an important "learning period" during which you should encourage chewing, even if there are no visible teeth. Switch to chunkier foods — either commercial junior foods or your own food blended less smoothly. Just be sure all the chunks are small and soft enough to not cause choking if swallowed whole.

Around ten months of age your baby will be ready to handle a spoon some of the time, although she won't have the wrist control yet to get much into her mouth. Let her feed herself small chunks of food with her fingers. She's now into the transition period, covered in the next chapter.

If Your Baby Is Choking

1. Lay your baby face down on your forearm with his head slightly lower. Support the baby firmly by holding your arm close to your body or on your knee. Give four good whacks with the heel of your hand on his back between the shoulder blades.
2. If that doesn't work, turn the infant over and lay him on his back on a firm surface. Deliver four rapid upward chest thrusts, over the sternum (where the rib cage meets), using two fingers.
3. If breathing has still not resumed, tilt his head back, and pull the lower jaw forward. That pulls the tongue out of the way and helps open the airway. Look down his throat for the foreign body. If you can see it, you can put your finger down his throat and try to dislodge it. But be careful, you don't want to shove the food further down. (Don't put your fingers into his throat blindly.)
4. If breathing still hasn't started, try to resuscitate with four breaths by mouth-to-mouth or mouth-to-mouth-and-nose technique.
5. Keep repeating these four steps while trying to get medical help.

If the Choking Victim Is an Older Child

1. You can use a modified Heimlich maneuver. Lay the child on his back; kneel next to him and place the heel of *one* hand on the child's stomach midway between the belly button and rib cage. Administer a series of six to ten rapid inward and upward thrusts.
2. If the obstruction is not relieved, open the child's mouth by lifting the jaw forward and look for the obstruction. If you can see it, you can try to remove it with your finger. Again, be careful not to push the obstruction further in by blindly stabbing at it.
3. If the child is still not breathing, attempt artificial respiration, then repeat abdominal thrusts, while calling for help.

Before the situation occurs, parents and caregivers should ask their physician to demonstrate the above techniques.

Weaning to a Cup

You can start introducing your baby to a cup at about four to five months of age. By then she'll be taking fruit juices and water, and the cup can be used from the start to serve them. You can even put a little of her formula or some of your expressed breast-milk in the cup. When you are doing the serving, it will be easier to use a clear plastic glass so you can see how fast she is drinking. Later, when she wants to grab the cup from you, a two-handled baby cup with a lid, spout and weighted bottom helps reduce the number of spills.

Starting Regular Milk

Regular cow's milk shouldn't be given to babies under six months of age. It's not nutritionally balanced for the human infant and can cause gastrointestinal bleeding or kidney damage. But once your infant is nine to twelve months old and eating a variety of other foods to balance his diet, whole cow's milk can be used.

If you're using formula in a bottle, you can switch to whole milk in the bottle at this time. Two percent or skim milk is not recommended as your baby needs the essential fat in whole milk at this stage.

Believe it or not, fat is an essential nutrient. Most adults eat too much fat, but infants need the fat in milk. It contains an essential fatty acid that is necessary for growth as part of the structure of cells. Moreover, some babies develop chronic diarrhea when their diet is too low in fat. Also, because reduced fat milks have fewer calories, the infant may drink more milk to obtain the same energy. That can start a habit of stretched stomach and overeating.

Just because your baby is drinking regular milk from a cup at mealtime doesn't mean you have to stop nursing or giving your baby a bottle some of the time. There's nothing wrong with continuing to nurse once or twice a day as long as you are both enjoying the experience. Your milk supply may decrease, but your baby can still enjoy the comfort of your breast. If you try to rush giving up the nipple or bottle, you may start a thumb-sucking habit. It is possible that your youngster may like that bedtime feed so much he wants to breast-feed until school age. The habit won't harm him; you may or may not feel comfortable with this option.

4

SOME COMMON CONCERNS WHEN FEEDING BABIES

Feeding-related problems — from colic and constipation to rashes and rejection — can be very disconcerting for babies and parents. No one likes to see a baby fuss, cry or suffer. And within a very short time, a minor problem can become severe.

The advice in this chapter is a place to start. However, I urge you to discuss with your doctor any feeding problems or concerns. Don't try to diagnose problems yourself.

Botulism

Botulism is a type of food poisoning, usually associated with contaminated canned food. But there is a rare form of botulism that can occur in infants given honey or corn syrup in foods or formula, or on a pacifier. This condition is serious and can be fatal. Therefore, Health and Welfare Canada recommends that infants under twelve months of age *not* be given honey or corn syrup.

Celiac Disease

Celiac disease occurs in some babies who cannot digest the protein in wheat, rye, oats and barley. The symptoms are frequent, foul-smelling, frothy bowel movements. Talk to your doctor if your baby's dirty diapers appear unusual, especially after you've started feeding her cereals. Your doctor or a dietitian can prescribe a special diet if this is the case (see Chapter Thirteen).

Chubby Babies

Any parent who battles the bulge herself worries that her baby will inherit the same heartache. It doesn't help to read articles that say, "Fat babies will become overweight children and then obese adults." Fortunately recent studies have shown that fat infants are not destined to remain fat, and most adult obesity cannot be explained by obesity in infancy. Also, there is no proof that breast-feeding prevents obesity or that early introduction of solid foods causes obesity.

If your baby looks a little chubby, don't panic. It may be that he is laying down reserves, ready for the next growth spurt. A protruding stomach is normal at this age.

That doesn't mean you should overfeed your baby. Ask your doctor to show you how your baby has been progressing relative to average growth rates. Babies who are both longer and heavier than average are just fine — as are babies who are short and light. The time to take action is when height and weight gains are out-of-sync with each other.

If your doctor does agree that your baby is putting on the pounds too quickly, think about your feeding style. Are you misinterpreting every cry as a hunger cry? Are you offering milk when water is all that's needed? Are you serving too much solid food? An overfed baby can easily become thirsty, but the need is for plain water, not more juice or milk.

In babies, as well as adults, excessive weight gain can be the result of too little activity, rather than too much food. Is your baby restricted to the playpen for long periods of time? Maybe he just needs more opportunity to crawl about and explore his environment. My son looked too fat at six months. Six weeks later, after he'd learned to crawl, he was skinny.

Colds or Teething

Often the very first sign that your baby is developing a cold or illness, or is teething, will be a missed meal or two. Don't be concerned if he's off his food for a day or so. If fluids are all your baby wants, that's fine. Once he feels better you can be sure his appetite will be vigorous.

Colic

Infantile colic does exist. It's not all in your mind. Your baby may have sudden attacks of pain; her abdomen becomes distended and tense; she flexes or draws up her legs and arches her back; and she'll cry for long periods of time — usually between six and ten at night.

Review your feeding technique with your doctor. Are you overfeeding or underfeeding? If breast-feeding, could it be something you've eaten that's bothering your baby? If bottle-feeding, your doctor may suggest a change in formula. When nothing else works, you may have to resign yourself to walking the floor with the baby for several hours every evening as medications rarely work. Understanding spouses and friends are most helpful, as is the knowledge that this condition will resolve itself spontaneously by the fourth month of age.

Constipation

Constipation probably won't be a problem as long as breast-milk is the sole food. Older breast-fed babies may not have a bowel movement every day, but the stool isn't hard or difficult to pass. However, bottle-fed babies may need extra water first thing in the morning and between feedings to prevent hard, dry stools. Regularity is difficult to define — it may be once every two to three days for one baby, and twice a day for another.

Once your baby starts eating a few solids, the character of the stools will change. Too much rice cereal can cause constipation. Just cut back on the cereal and use more puréed fruit — applesauce or prune juice. Laxatives, suppositories or enemas are generally too harsh for babies. Don't use them without your doctor's recommendation.

Diarrhea

Very loose, watery bowel movements can be an early sign of illness or teething, a symptom of food allergy, or a reaction to spoiled food. Diarrhea that continues for more than a day can have severe consequences. Your baby is losing essential body fluids; contact your doctor. He'll likely want to see the baby and will recommend extra fluids — breast-milk, water or diluted formula or juice (half water, half juice or formula). Rice cereal often helps to prevent loose stools and bananas may be recommended to replace important minerals lost during diarrhea.

Soft drinks, tea, rice water, undiluted fruit juices or fruit drinks, bouillon or boiled skim milk are *not* appropriate treatments for a baby with diarrhea. Commercial oral rehydration products should be used *only* if your doctor recommends them.

And beware of some of the "grandmother" treatments. Prolonged use of limited diets, such as the BRAT diet for diarrhea — bananas, rice, applesauce and tea or toast — have caused greater problems than they've solved. When used for a long period of time, such diets have caused malnutrition with associated chronic diarrhea. It used to be the style to take babies off milk during a severe bout of illness. But that treatment is quickly losing favor as well.

Once your child is ready to start eating a normal diet offer smaller, more frequent meals until he seems to be back to normal.

Gas

Swallowing too much air, drinking too fast, overfeeding, or starting on solids too early can all cause a baby's tummy to become bloated and unsettled. Maybe you need to burp your baby more frequently during feedings. Or maybe your milk supply is flowing too quickly at the beginning of the feed. Try expressing a little of the excess milk before putting your baby on your breast.

Some vegetables such as peas and corn can cause gas if served too often. Review your infant's menu if this is a problem.

Jaundice

A small proportion of babies (one to two percent) develop breast-milk jaundice soon after birth. At first they look like they have a sun tan, but later their skin takes on a distinctive yellowish tinge. If jaundice is severe, your doctor may want you to discontinue breast-feeding for a few days. If you wish to continue nursing, pump your breast-milk and discard it during this time.

Rashes or Hives

A mild pimply rash that looks like adolescent acne but occurs at about one month of age is probably a sign of clogged pores. Keep your baby's face well washed and lightly powdered with cornstarch to dry up excess oil.

Other rashes, however, can be a sign of a food sensitivity. Remove any new foods introduced in the last week from the diet until the rash disappears. You can try the offending food again in a month or so.

Refusing Foods

Relax. Babies rarely starve themselves. It's very likely that a food refused today will be eagerly enjoyed next week — or next month. Force feeding can start a vicious cycle — the child enjoys the extra attention, while the parents become more frustrated. No one gains. If your baby doesn't seem to be eating enough, you may be overestimating your baby's appetite and energy needs.

Spitting Up

Hungry babies sometimes gulp down more than their stomach can handle, then spit up the excess. (Spitting up, or regurgitation involves small amounts of food; vomiting is the forceful expulsion of large amounts of liquid or food.) Spitting up probably hurts your clothes more than the baby. To reduce the problem, slow down the feeding; burp your baby halfway through; feed small portions more frequently; avoid excitement and activity after feeds; lay your baby on her stomach, rather than propping her up after a meal.

Underweight

"Failure to thrive" is the term doctors use for a baby that is not gaining weight. But such babies are the exception, not the rule. Look at your baby's growth chart. Is he gaining, slowly but steadily? Is he alert much of the day, lively and active? Are you offering the appropriate foods — milk and manageable solids? If you answer yes to all of these, chances are your child is growing at a rate that's normal for him. But if you are concerned, speak to your doctor. A professional will be able to tell at a glance if your baby is adequately nourished.

Vomiting

Vomiting and fever are more serious in babies than in adults. If your baby is vomiting, contact your doctor, and in the meantime, offer only fluids — water and juice if she'll take them. Sometimes, though, fluids just stimulate more vomiting. In that case, limit drinking to small sips. Although loss of body salts (electrolytes) is serious, don't try to replace them yourself. If electrolyte replacement is necessary, leave it up to your doctor.

5

TRANSITION TO TABLE FOODS
Ten to Twenty-Four Months

In the last three months before the milestone first birthday, your baby's participation in feeding will quickly change from passive to active. Where once he simply accepted or rejected food, he now actively participates in the feeding process. Important physical development milestones have made this possible.

- He has the hand coordination to reach for objects, stick a finger in a dish or in his mouth.
- With a proficient thumb-forefinger pinch, he can pick up bite-sized pieces of food.
- He points to the foods he wants, and may even be able to vocalize choices.
- Wrist action necessary for good control of the spoon and cup will continue to improve during this second year.
- Now that he sits alone, without support and for longer periods of time, self-feeding is easier.
- When drinking he takes three or four swallows in sequence.
- With his jaw, he can munch and mash soft lumps of food, whether or not he has teeth.

- He uses his tongue to push food from side to side in his mouth, making swallowing control better.

Increase Variety

At this stage, offer your baby increasing variety in taste, texture and temperature. Commercial junior foods are a way to start, but by about seven or eight months of age you'll find that many of the cooked vegetables, soft fruits and ground meats you're preparing for the rest of the family can be mashed for baby.

Pasta wheels, shells, tubes and twists, or small elbow macaroni with a cheese and tomato sauce are favorite finger foods — even if they are messy. Once your baby is a year old, whole egg dishes — hard-cooked or soft-boiled egg, scrambled egg, omelette, quiche, soufflé, French toast, fried egg sandwich — can become regular items on the menu. Eggs are an excellent source of protein and iron, essential nutrients at this age. And unless your family has a history of cholesterol problems, you needn't worry about baby's dietary cholesterol intake.

Easy Cheese Soufflé

1 tsp	butter or margarine, softened	5 mL
1	slice whole wheat or white bread	1
¼ cup	grated Cheddar cheese	50 mL
1	egg	1
¼ cup	milk	50 mL
Pinch	dry mustard	Pinch

Spread butter on bread and cut into small cubes. In a large, lightly greased custard cup, alternate layers of bread cubes and cheese. In a bowl, beat together egg, milk and dry mustard; pour over bread; stir gently. Let stand for at least 10 minutes.

Bake in a 350°F (180°C) oven for 25 minutes, or until set in center. Turn soufflé out of baking dish; serve warm.

Microwave: Microwave on HIGH (100%) for 1 minute; stir gently. Microwave on MEDIUM (50%) for 3 ½-4 minutes; let stand 2 minutes.

Yield: one ½-cup (125-mL) serving.

Easy Family-Sized Cheese Soufflé: Multiply all ingredients by 6 using ½ tsp (2 mL) dry mustard. Assemble according to directions above. Bake in a 350°F (180°C) oven for 40-45 minutes, or until set in center.

Microwave cooking is not recommended for family-sized soufflé.

Yield: 4-6 servings.

Maple French Toast Sticks

This can be a finger food for small children as the maple flavoring and sweetness are in the toast coating and therefore not as messy to eat. When served to older children capable of handling forks and knives, the sticks are simpler to cut.

2-3	slices French or whole wheat bread (slices should be ¾ in. (1.5 cm) thick)	2-3
2 tbsp	all-purpose flour	25 mL
1	large egg	1
2 tbsp	evaporated milk or light cream	25 mL
1 tbsp	maple syrup	15 mL
Pinch	cinnamon, optional	Pinch

Cut 8 bread sticks of approximately ¾ in. (1.5 cm) thick. (If desired, trim off crisp or tough crusts, crumble and use in another recipe.) Coat bread sticks with flour. In a shallow bowl or pie plate, beat egg, evaporated milk, syrup and cinnamon, if desired, until frothy. Place bread sticks in egg mixture, turning to thoroughly coat all sides.

Lightly grease a heated griddle. A few drops of water sprinkled on griddle should bounce and sizzle when heat is just right. Cook coated bread sticks on griddle, over medium heat, until golden brown on all sides.

TIP: Day-old or slightly stale bread works best in this recipe.
Yield: 8 sticks.

Regular meats such as chicken, pork, lamb and steak will continue to be difficult to chew until the molars come in. Even when you cut the meat very finely, your baby can't grind it further. One baby I know keeps shoving bits of meat into her mouth until she gags, so continue to use your blender, food processor or grinder for her meats.

Probably the easiest meats to use are the cured hams and bolognas. But limit these meats to a maximum of one or two servings a week as most cured meats are high in saturated fat, not the kind baby needs, as well as being high in sodium-containing compounds (e.g., salt). Your infant gets plenty of sodium from her milk. Her immature kidneys cannot handle an excess of it.

When the family meat dish isn't appropriate, serve baked beans, eggs, or canned, fresh or frozen fish instead. Bake or poach fish rather than frying it, and be sure to remove all the bones. Legumes are also a good source of protein, B vitamins and iron, and are soft to chew.

Toddler Fish

| ½ lb | frozen cod, halibut or sole, partially thawed and cut into cubes | 250 g |
| 2 tbsp | very finely chopped celery | 25 mL |

¼ cup	milk	50 mL
3 tbsp	dry bread crumbs	45 mL
¼ cup	grated Cheddar cheese	50 mL

In a small saucepan, combine fish, celery and milk. Bring just to a boil; cover, reduce heat and simmer for 5-7 minutes or until a fork easily penetrates fish. Sprinkle with bread crumbs and top with cheese; cover and let stand on warm range element for 2-3 minutes, or until cheese melts. Serve warm.

Microwave: In a small casserole, combine fish, celery and milk. Cover with waxed paper and microwave on HIGH (100%) for 3 minutes; let stand 2 minutes. Stir fish mixture. Sprinkle with bread crumbs and top with cheese. Microwave on MEDIUM-HIGH (70%) for 2 minutes; let stand 1 minute. Serve warm.
Yield: two ¾-cup (175-mL) servings.

(If you are not serving two children, you can refrigerate and save one serving for the next day. Thawing and refreezing fish is not recommended.)

Commercial Foods for Older Babies

Heinz has several "Good 'n' Chunky" dinners and Gerber has microwaveable "Graduate" meals aimed at the twelve- to eighteen-month-old baby. These transition meals have more texture than junior foods, but still can be safely gummed by babies who don't have many teeth. You won't need to use them all the time, but they are a handy alternative when the family dinner isn't appropriate for your baby.

By this age many babies balk at infant cereals, but they still need the extra iron. Heinz "Nutrios," a ready-to-eat cereal that children can eat with their fingers, is fortified with plenty of easily absorbed iron. The cereals older children and adults enjoy contain much less iron and in a form that may not be as easily absorbed. They are not as good choices for babies under two.

Eating Skills

When serving your baby messier food — his cereal, for instance — let him have a spoon too. No doubt he'll first succeed in putting more on his chin, chest and you than in his mouth. But if he has a chance to persevere, he'll soon get the idea.

Babies learn by imitation, not by instruction. Allow him to eat even messy food with his fingers, but offer a spoon each time. By watching the rest of the family, he'll soon learn to copy your choice of utensil. His spoon should have a wide, short handle for easier manipulation. And he'll need a dish with straight sides that doesn't slide all over the tray as he struggles to shove the food onto his spoon.

Appetite Drops Off at Twelve Months

Around the first birthday, just when you think feeding babies is easy, your baby's appetite will dramatically decrease. Her growth rate is now slower. During the first year her birth weight tripled, but it won't quadruple until her second birthday.

The next six months are a time for mastering social and motor skills — learning to talk and walk. During mealtime she'll be easily distracted; she'll be busy noticing what's happening around her and will be less interested in focusing on the task of eating.

Mealtime can be frustrating for parents. One meal she'll be hungry; the next meal she won't eat anything. Food will be wasted. You can keep waste to a minimum by always starting with *very* small portions. Expect a one-year-old to eat about a third of what you eat — a third of a sandwich, three or four ounces of milk, a tablespoon of potato, half an ounce of cheese. Parents often find they're gaining weight eating all the leftovers even if they never prepare lunch for themselves.

Sample Menu Pattern for a One-Year-Old

Breakfast:	¼ cup (50 mL)	infant or toddler cereal
	½ cup (125 mL)	homo or 2% milk (some on cereal)
	1	small boiled egg
	½ slice	whole wheat toast
	½ tsp (2 mL)	butter or margarine
Snack:	½ cup (125 mL)	orange juice
Lunch:	¼ cup (50 mL)	cottage cheese
	1-2 tbsp (25 mL)	cooked carrots
	½ slice	whole wheat bread
	½ cup (125 mL)	homo or 2% milk
	⅓	banana
Snack:	½ oz (15 g)	cheese
	2	crackers
Dinner:	1½ oz (45 g)	diced chicken
	1-2 tbsp (25 mL)	mashed potato
	½ tsp (2 mL)	butter or margarine
	1-2 tbsp (25 mL)	green beans
	½ cup (125 mL)	milk pudding
	½ cup (125 mL)	milk
Before Bed:	½	apple

Introducing New Foods

Studies show that seventy-seven percent of children between the ages of one and two will try a new food. But that adventuresome spirit drops to ten percent for two- to four-year-olds, and only seven percent in the junior kindergarten years. I wonder why children become so suspicious?

Until we have the answers, my advice is to introduce as many new tastes, textures and combinations as possible between the first and second birthday.

When you are introducing a new food:

- Introduce only one new food at a meal, preferably along with a favorite food.
- Offer only a small portion — for tasting — ideally at the beginning of the meal.
- Expect your child to like the food; show you like it.
- Don't be concerned if the new food is rejected; just withdraw it without comment. You can offer it again several days later, without reminding her of the initial refusal.
- Don't expect consistency; a food that's disliked today may be greeted with enthusiasm next week.
- The comfort of familiar foods is more appropriate when your child is ill or irritable.

Preschoolers don't respond well to reasoning, coaxing, threats, bribes or punishment to entice them to eat. If you use those techniques, you may win in the short term, but your child loses in the long run. He is far less likely to return to a food he was forced to eat.

Manners Can Wait

- It's not uncommon for children at this age to have difficulty chewing small pieces of meat. If they spit it out, it's not bad manners, just a way to prevent gagging. Have a washcloth or paper towel handy, and clean up the mess without comment.
- Children are learning social responses. They'll soon realize that if they stop eating, or throw food, it attracts mom

and dad's attention. The more attention they get, the more the behavior is being rewarded. If spills are just quietly cleaned up, the behavior is not as likely to become intentional.

- Several dishes on the table or tray at once are confusing. One food at a time is easiest to handle and you'll save many spills. Withhold milk or bread until after most of the main course is finished. After your child has had a chance to drink, remove the milk again before the dessert course. You can always offer the cup at the end of the meal.
- Prepare for spills. A dropcloth or newspapers under the high chair and a large bib is nouveau-baby fashionable.

Mealtimes

This is a time to be very flexible about the time of day for meals. When your baby is ready to give up his morning nap, you may find him nodding off in his high chair at noon. Better to skip his morning snack, and let him eat at 11:00 to 11:30 A.M. Similarly, waiting for 6:00 P.M. dinner may be impossible.

Even if he has his dinner before you, let your baby climb back into his high chair when you eat. Put a few bits of cooked carrot, some peas, or chunks of peach on his tray for another mini-meal. This is the way he'll learn family eating routines.

With all these extra meals, it's no wonder that parents and caregivers looking after school-aged children as well feel they are never out of the kitchen. A microwave oven can be a real timesaver for warming last night's leftovers, or cooking a few beans and carrots. But be careful. Small servings can overcook or quickly become too hot for young children. *Continue to stir and test all foods heated in a microwave before serving them to your child.*

Beverages

If you're worried that your baby isn't drinking enough milk, remember she needs less; after the first birthday sixteen ounces a day is adequate. Milk is nature's "almost perfect" food. It is an excellent source of protein, vitamins A, D and riboflavin, and the mineral calcium. But milk does not provide all the necessary vitamins and minerals for growing children. Therefore, your child can overdo a good thing. Too much milk can interfere with her appetite for other nutritious foods.

If, however, she's not drinking all the milk she needs, some of the daily servings can be offered in other ways:

- hard cheeses, cottage cheese or yogurt
- on cereals
- in cream soups
- in milk puddings — bread pudding, rice pudding, tapioca pudding, junket and custards

An economical way to add extra milk goodness is to add some skim milk powder when you are cooking hot cereals or preparing meat loaves.

Sometimes all she wants to drink is juice. Too much juice can contribute to diarrhea, and she can get all the vitamin C she needs from just two or three ounces of juice daily. If you allow fruit juices at meals or snack time without limit, you could destroy her appetite for other foods. At the very least, you'll have to change frequent dirty diapers. So if she repeatedly asks for juice, offer her diluted juice, water or milk. If her thirst is genuine, she'll give in. Often, a request for a drink is a request for a new activity or some attention.

Foods to Chew On

Once the gums become hard, even before the first teeth erupt, baby is ready for something to chew on. Plain dried bread, teething biscuits, and soft (not crumbly) toast are easy choices as table foods.

After she's a year old, use fruits such as banana, ripe peach, steamed apple slices (without the skin), and vegetables — cooked carrot or turnip slices that are soft enough so she won't choke, slices of hard-cooked egg, boiled potato chunks (without the skin) and cubes of cheese are good choices.

Foods to Delay

Don't offer celery sticks and raw vegetables until your baby is at least eighteen months old and chewing properly. Otherwise he might bite off and swallow a piece that could become stuck in his throat. Some of the ready-to-eat cereals can also cause choking if swallowed without chewing. Kids at this age love grapes. To make them safe to eat, cut them in quarters and remove the seeds.

Nuts, chips, popcorn and candies are not appropriate for babies under four years of age. Surprisingly, wieners are responsible for more asphyxiation deaths than any other food. That's because a piece of wiener is just the right shape to plug the throat. If you are serving wieners to your family and want to include baby, be sure to cut his into lengthwise quarters before cutting crosswise.

Peanut butter can also cause problems. Served on it's own, it can stick to a child's vocal cords; spread thinly on bread or toast, it's fine.

Watch Her Siblings

Many feeding problems occur when an older sibling shares her food. In a recent medical journal, a pediatrician wrote about a nine-month-old girl who had red, swollen, hard patches on her cheeks. The patches were similar to those seen in babies after exposure to severe cold. But this was the middle of July! It seems that the baby's five-year-old brother had held a popsicle in his sister's mouth for about ten minutes. The type of fat under the skin in newborns solidifies at higher temperatures than the fat of older children, creating red, warm irritated patches.

The safest advice is:

- Make sure an adult is present whenever your baby is being fed.
- Discourage other youngsters from feeding your baby without your permission.
- Limit eating to times when the child is sitting.

Problems are more likely to occur if the child nibbles while carrying food about.

That last bit of advice will also save your carpets and furniture from many messes.

6

FLOWERING INDEPENDENCE
Two-Year-Olds

By the end of the second year, your toddler has improved wrist dexterity, so eating by himself is much easier. He can probably graduate to a broad-mouthed cup without a spout and a short-handled fork. Continue to encourage this independence, even if it means occasional spills and accidents. Help only when requested.

I'm reminded of a neighbor's boy who would revert from independent eating to helplessness whenever his grandmother walked in. Kevin knew she loved feeding him and he wasn't about to lose any opportunity for extra attention. Yet between Nanny's visits, Kevin's mother was able to leave him to his own devices at feeding time, and he became very competent with a spoon and fork.

Eating will be much easier if your youngster can reach the table easily and still have his feet firmly planted. If the high chair is considered too babyish, or is needed for a new arrival, you might want to try a low table and chair beside yours. If you're choosing a booster seat, buy or build one that allows room for him to rest his feet on the chair.

Continue to place just one course at a time in front of your child; it's less confusing for him this way, and there will be fewer spills.

Favorite Foods

At two-and-a-half years, all twenty baby teeth will probably be in. Once your child can chew, she may prefer certain vegetables raw — carrot and turnip sticks, cauliflower and broccoli flowerets, cucumber wedges, lettuce and cabbage salads. The taste is milder if not cooked. Remember she could still easily choke; do stay with her at mealtime.

For main dishes, the favorites are still warm, moist, soft-textured foods. In addition to the old standbys — hamburger, macaroni and cheese (see Chapter Eight for some variations), spaghetti with meat sauce — try the following recipes.

Tuna Cheese Open-Faced Sandwich

1	7-oz/198-g can tuna, flaked and drained	1
2	hard-cooked eggs, finely chopped	2
½ cup	diced processed-cheese food	125 mL
1 tbsp	sweet relish	15 mL
¼ cup	mayonnaise or salad dressing	50 mL
4	English muffins, split and lightly toasted	4
	Stuffed olives, sliced	

Combine tuna, eggs, cheese, relish and mayonnaise. Spoon filling on each muffin half. Heat under broiler for about 1 minute, until cheese starts to melt; do not brown. Garnish with olive slices.

Microwave: Place the dressed muffin halves on a microwave rack or paper towel. Microwave on MEDIUM-HIGH (70%) for 45 seconds, or until cheese starts to melt. Garnish as above. *Yield:* 4-6 servings.

Tofu Finger Snacks

These are designed as savory snacks and should have appeal to the "fried food" generation. Tofu, an excellent source of protein, can be flavored with almost any favorite seasoning. Those who like Chinese food can sprinkle the pressed tofu with soy sauce. To add chicken flavor, press the tofu a little longer and sprinkle with concentrated (canned) chicken broth before coating. For these flavor variations, substitute a whole egg beaten with a little milk for the spaghetti sauce.

4 oz	water-packed tofu (¼ of 500-g package)	125 g
1	egg yolk	1
¼ cup	spaghetti sauce, ketchup or barbecue sauce	50 mL
½ cup	dry bread crumbs	125 mL
1 tbsp	finely grated Parmesan or old Cheddar cheese, optional	15 mL
	All-purpose flour	

Cut tofu into two slices, each about ¾ in. (2 cm) thick. Make a stack of 8 paper towels, each folded in half; place tofu slices in center of stack. Gently but firmly press tofu until towels are thoroughly soaked. Discard towels and cut tofu into 18 cubes, each about ¾ in. (2 cm) square.

In a bowl, beat egg yolk and spaghetti sauce; combine bread crumbs and cheese, if desired. Coat tofu cubes with flour, dip in sauce mixture, then coat thoroughly with crumbs. Place on a lightly greased baking sheet. Bake in a 375°F (190°C) oven for 12-15 minutes, or until golden brown. Cool slightly. Serve warm as finger food.

Yield: about 18 cubes.

Raspberry Jellied Dessert

2	envelopes unflavored gelatin	2
¾ cup	milk	175 mL
1 cup	boiling water	250 mL
1 tbsp	lemon juice	15 mL
1	15-oz/425-g package frozen raspberries in light syrup, partly thawed	1
	Fresh raspberries, optional	

Sprinkle gelatin over cold milk in food processor or blender. Let stand until gelatin is softened. Add boiling water. Cover and blend until gelatin is completely dissolved, about 1 minute. Add lemon juice and raspberries. Blend until smooth. Pour into a 4-cup (1-L) greased mold. Refrigerate until set, 1-2 hours. Before serving, unmold and garnish with fresh raspberries, if desired.

TIP: Substitute strawberries for raspberries. Or substitute ¾ cup (450 mL) sliced and lightly sweetened fresh raspberries or strawberries.

Yield: five ½-cup (125-mL) servings.

Sips and Tastes

Peter was a sickly baby. In the first year he had to be hospitalized more than once in order for the doctors to investigate a digestive problem. Weight gain became an important issue at every doctor's visit. His mother became concerned that if he didn't continue to gain he would be hospitalized again. She watched over every

bite he ate, coaxed him to finish meals and catered to
his food whims. But still he seemed to eat like a bird.
By the time he was three even his grandmother refused
to babysit for him over mealtime.

Children will not go hungry for long. But if you've made a habit of coaxing, refusing to eat becomes a way to get attention. To break the routine, Peter's mother had to accept the fact that Peter knew better than she did how much to eat. She had to stop the mealtime manipulations; serve him his meal, then remove the leftovers (without comment) after a reasonable period of time. If he went to bed hungry for a few nights, he'd soon learn there was a new game plan.

Think Small

Throughout the toddler period, appetites continue to be un-predictable — meal to meal and day to day. This is the time to buy the smallest apples and pears.

Don't judge nutritional adequacy by one meal, or one day. And don't judge child-sized portions by your normal serving sizes. Toddler portions are much smaller.

You need an overall picture. For one week keep a diary of everything your toddler eats — and what you eat. Then compare it to the suggested number and size of servings on the next page. Each day, your toddler needs a variety of foods: grains, vegetables and fruit, milk or milk products, and meat or alternatives. These are the food groups in Canada's Food Guide to Healthy Eating.

The number and size of servings in Canada's Food Guide to Healthy Eating (see pages 204 and 205) make it an appropriate guide for people over the age of four. The menu plan on the next page is a modification, more applicable to the serving sizes and appetites of small children.

Eating Pattern for Preschoolers
two to four years of age

Grain Products
5-7 portions daily
e.g., $\frac{1}{2}$-1 slice bread
50-125 mL ($\frac{1}{4}$-$\frac{1}{2}$ cup) cooked cereal
75-200 mL ($\frac{1}{3}$-$\frac{3}{4}$ cup) cold cereal
$\frac{1}{4}$-$\frac{1}{2}$ roll, bun, bagel or muffin
75-200 mL ($\frac{1}{3}$-$\frac{3}{4}$ cup) cooked rice, macaroni, spaghetti or noodles

Meat & Alternatives
2-3 portions daily
e.g., 30-60 g (1-2 oz) cooked lean meat, fish or poultry
15 mL (1 tbsp) peanut butter
50-125 mL ($\frac{1}{4}$-$\frac{1}{2}$ cup) cooked peas, beans or lentils
$\frac{1}{2}$-1 egg
50-100 g (2-3$\frac{1}{2}$ oz) tofu

Vegetables & Fruit
4-8 portions daily
e.g., 50-75 mL ($\frac{1}{4}$-$\frac{1}{3}$ cup) vegetables or fruit
$\frac{1}{2}$-1 small potato, carrot, tomato, peach, apple, orange or banana
75-125 mL ($\frac{1}{3}$-$\frac{1}{2}$ cup) juice

Milk or Milk Products
4-6 portions daily
e.g., 125-200 mL ($\frac{1}{2}$-$\frac{3}{4}$ cup) milk
75-125 mL ($\frac{1}{3}$-$\frac{1}{2}$ cup) yogurt
20-30 g ($\frac{3}{4}$-1 oz) cheese
75-125 mL ($\frac{1}{3}$-$\frac{1}{2}$ cup) milk pudding

Did your toddler have at least the minimum number of servings from each food group? The chart on the next page shows one mother's record of her son's eating pattern over the course of a day.

Foods and beverages that are not part of any food group can be used in moderate amounts when making meals and snacks. Remember to serve water often to satisfy thirst.

Sample Menu Pattern

Nathan two and a half years old	Grains	Vegetables & Fruit	Milk Products	Meat & Alternatives	Other Foods
Breakfast					
½ orange in sections		1			
4 Maple French Toast Sticks with syrup (recipe, p. 75)	1		1		1
¼ cup (50 mL) applesauce		1			
¼ cup (50 mL) whole milk			½		
Morning Snack					
1 slice fruit bread with honey	1				1
⅓ cup (75 mL) whole milk			1		
Lunch					
½ cup (125 mL) baked beans				1	
½ tomato, sliced		1			
¼ whole wheat roll with margarine	1				1
⅓ cup (75 mL) canned peaches		1			
½ cup (125 mL) whole milk			1		
Afternoon Snack:					
½ banana		1			
2 crackers with cheese spread	1		½		
Dinner					
1½ oz (45 g) baked fish				1	
⅓ cup (75 mL) squash		1			
¼ cup (50 mL) zucchini coins		1			
⅓ cup (75 mL) rice pudding	½		½		
½ cup (125 mL) whole milk			1		
Before Bed					
⅓ cup (75 mL) cold cereal with ¼ cup (50 mL) whole milk	1		½		
Total for Day	5½	7	6	2	3

If you and your toddler are usually eating enough foods from each food group in a twenty-four-hour period, but are still hungry, then you can add more — larger or more servings of favorite foods from the food groups, butter or margarine in moderation, or the occasional cookie or ice cream treat.

But if meals are mostly wasted, then consider the quantity and type of food he eats as snacks. Many traditional snack foods — potato chips, cookies, chocolate bars — are very high in calories and fat. They are not appropriate for preschool children who must get their full day's supply of protein, vitamins and minerals in about 1100 to 1300 calories.

Snacks

Two- and three-year-olds have small tummies so snacks may be necessary mini-meals. Otherwise, it would be difficult for them to eat enough in a three-meal-a-day pattern to meet their energy needs. But remember your toddler's weight is less than a quarter of yours. That means, a couple of crackers for him an hour before dinner is equivalent to eight or more cookies for you. What would that do to your appetite?

You'll also want to choose snacks with an eye to protecting baby teeth from dental decay.

Here's How Decay Is Caused

Each time teeth are exposed to sugar, bacteria that are always in the mouth have a meal. As these bacteria grow and multiply, they produce acid. It's this acid bath that eats away at tooth enamel, causing cavities.

$$\text{SUGAR} + \text{BACTERIA} = \text{ACID}$$
$$\text{ACID} + \text{TOOTH} \quad = \text{DECAY}$$

But if there is sufficient time between acid attacks, the saliva can neutralize the acid, and minerals in the saliva can repair the tooth damage. This is the situation when sweet foods are eaten only at mealtimes. But if your child has sweets between meals, there isn't time for repair. The frequent acid attacks gradually lead to decay of the tooth enamel. Bedtime or evening snacks are the most damaging of all because the saliva flow is less during sleep.

Most foods, including fruit, juice, crackers, bread and milk contain sugar or starch that can be turned into sugar. There are, however, some foods that are worse than others. Anything that sticks in the crevices between the teeth — candies, suckers, raisins, honey with peanut butter, chewy granola bars, chewy cookies — provides the longest acid attack. Foods that stimulate saliva flow, such as cheese, or are liquid themselves — fruit, juice and milk — are more quickly washed away.

When a nutritious between-meal snack is appropriate, try these good dental snacks:

- white milk
- cheese chunks
- plain yogurt
- cottage cheese
- bread or rolls
- muffins
- steamed vegetable sticks (raw if she can chew well)
- pieces of fruit
- slices of hard-cooked egg
- peanut butter on crackers
- fruit and vegetable juices
- fruit juice popsicle (recipe below)

Frozen Yogurt Pops

2 cups	plain yogurt	500 mL
¾ cup	frozen concentrated orange juice, thawed	175 mL
2	egg whites	2
1 tbsp	sugar	15 mL

Combine yogurt and concentrated orange juice. Beat egg whites until frothy. Add sugar gradually (it's very little) and beat until firm. Fold into orange mixture. Pour into 18 individual popsicle containers and freeze until firm. (If you don't have popsicle containers, use ice cube trays and insert a popsicle stick into each square.)
Yield: 18 pops.

Tooth Care

Children need all twenty primary teeth for eating and chewing, speaking and good looks. As well, baby teeth reserve a space in the jaw for the permanent teeth.

Although it may be too much to expect you to brush your toddler's teeth after every snack, you can encourage your child to rinse her mouth with water. After meals, you'll have to brush her teeth. A two-year-old can certainly handle a toothbrush, but she won't have the dexterity to do a thorough cleaning. Use a small brush with soft, polished bristles and a round end. You'll need to replace the brush every three or four months or as soon as the bristles become bent or frayed. Clean each tooth with an up-and-down action. Once a day, floss between the teeth as well.

By four or five, your child will be able to brush her own teeth, but you should be supervising the process until she's at least eight.

Breakfasts

I still believe that breakfast is the most important meal of the day, especially for children. You may not feel like eating with the birds, but your children may. Some children eat as much as half their daily energy intake at breakfast. In addition to calories, they need a balance of protein, vitamins and minerals to keep them alert and energetic for daytime activities.

Build their breakfast menu around a good protein source.

The traditional eggs cook quickly and can be served in a number of ways.

Dairy products are also a good source of protein. Milk on cereal is a start, but also consider cheese or yogurt for breakfast. The Danes have a good idea. They sprinkle ground rye bread on plain yogurt. (Use your food processor to grind the bread fine enough for your toddler.) The following recipe for homemade yogurt uses ultra-high-temperature (UHT) processed milk. With this milk you save the sterilizing step.

Homemade Yogurt

1	carton 2% UHT sterilized milk	1 L
½ cup	instant non-fat dry milk powder	125 mL
2 tbsp	fresh yogurt	25 mL
	or	
1	envelope (5 g) yogurt culture	1

In casserole, heat sterilized milk to 110°F (44°C). Stir in milk powder. Stir a small amount of warmed milk into fresh yogurt; stir into remaining milk in casserole. Transfer to large glass bowl. Cover with foil. Place in a warm place, not higher than 150°F (65°C), away from draft.

A warm oven is ideal for yogurt incubation: Heat oven to 200°F (100°C) for about 2 minutes. Turn oven off and cool to 150°F (65°C), 5-10 minutes. Turn oven light ON to maintain heat. Incubate milk mixture overnight (8-10 hours) or until yogurt is firm. Refrigerate until cool, about 2 hours, before serving.

TIP: The fresher the yogurt, the firmer it will be.

Yield: about 4 ½ cups (1 L).

Other possible breakfast protein sources include meat — even a slice of last night's meatloaf or a left-over chicken leg — and fish, a quick cooking option. And there's the old standby, peanut butter.

Breakfast can be the time for a daily vitamin C-containing food — any vitaminized fruit juice, the citrus fruits (oranges, grapefruit or tangerines) and their juices, and berries — strawberries, raspberries, blueberries and blackberries. Even cantaloupe and watermelon are a source of vitamin C.

For energy, B vitamins and iron, serve cereal (hot or cold), toast or muffins.

The following recipe for a fruit bread can be considered a complete instant breakfast. It provides fiber plus components from all four food groups, and gives the satisfaction of chewing which is missed in liquid breakfasts and supplements. It's made in a food processor so that the fruit and nuts are finely ground to avoid chewing and choking problems for young children. (If you don't have a food processor, chop the fruit and nuts, and use the recipe for older children and yourselves.)

Fruit Bonanza Bread

2¼ cups	whole wheat flour	550 mL
1 cup	instant non-fat dry milk powder	250 mL
½ cup	wheat germ	125 mL
¼ cup	lightly packed brown sugar	50 mL
¼ cup	oat bran	50 mL
1 tbsp	baking powder	15 mL
½ tsp	baking soda	2 mL
¼ tsp	salt	1 mL
¾ cup	dry roasted unsalted peanuts	175 mL
½ cup	pitted prunes	125 mL
½ cup	dried apricots	125 mL
1	large apple, cored and cut into chunks	1
½	large banana, cut into chunks	½

¾ cup	orange juice	175 mL
½ cup	vegetable oil	125 mL
½ cup	molasses	125 mL
3	eggs	3

Grease and line with greased waxed paper: two 8×4-in. (1.5-L) or 9×5-in. (2-L) loaf pans.

In a large bowl, combine flour, milk powder, wheat germ, brown sugar, oat bran, baking powder, baking soda and salt.

Insert metal blade in food processor. With motor running, add peanuts, prunes, apricots, apple and banana chunks; process until finely chopped. Scrape bowl; with motor running add orange juice, vegetable oil and molasses; process until well mixed. Add eggs; process just until well blended.

Add fruit mixture to dry ingredients, stirring by hand until well mixed. Spoon batter into prepared loaf pans.

Bake in a 325°F (160°C) oven 60-70 minutes, or until tester inserted in center comes out clean. Cool in pan 10 minutes. Remove and cool thoroughly. When cool, wrap tightly and store overnight to mellow flavors.

NOTE: This is a very moist bread. It is excellent toasted or warmed. It also freezes well.

Yield: 2 loaves.

FRUIT BREAD STICKS: As a teething food, cut cooled Fruit Bonanza Bread into thick sticks. Place sticks on cookie sheet. Bake in a 150°F (70°C) oven 15-25 minutes or until hard and crunchy. Store sticks in a tightly covered container in a dry place.

You'll notice my breakfast suggestions don't include doughnuts or sweet rolls. A sugar load on an empty stomach can give your children a quick energy boost, but it also stimulates an insulin response in their bodies. An hour or two later the insulin has helped transfer all the sugar into their cells. By mid-morning their blood sugar levels plummet; they run out of energy, and become tired and irritable.

But if breakfast is built around protein and starches (in cereal and bread), your children won't experience this yo-yo response in their blood sugar levels. During digestion, starches are broken down into sugars, but the absorption of sugar is much slower and more regulated. Protein can also be a source of blood sugar after absorption and metabolism.

That's not to say that a little jam or honey at breakfast is harmful. It just means sugar must be kept in balance.

The Noon Meal

Urban families often have just a light lunch at noon. But for toddlers, having the main meal at noon and a light supper often works better. Frequently young children are just too tired to eat well late in the day. With the following recipe you can turn a bowl of your child's favorite vegetable or cream soup into a main meal. These delicious miniature meatballs are the ideal size for little ones. It's easy to make large batches to have on hand. You can also serve the meatballs with heated canned spaghetti sauce or add them to commercial macaroni and cheese for quick, nutritious noontime meals.

Soup Balls

1	egg	1
1 tsp	Worcestershire sauce	5 mL
½ cup	instant non-fat dry milk powder	125 mL
¼ cup	wheat germ	50 mL
1 lb	lean ground beef, lamb or pork	450 g
2 tbsp	natural wheat bran, optional	25 mL

In a mixing bowl, beat egg and Worcestershire sauce. Stir in milk powder and wheat germ. Add ground meat and bran, if desired, mixing until very well blended. (Mixture is very thick; mix with clean hands if desired.)

Bring a large saucepan of water to a rolling boil. With two spoons, form miniature meatballs using about 1 tsp (5 mL) of mixture for each. Drop meatballs into boiling water. Meatballs float when cooked. Cook only a few meatballs at a time, so that water is at a constant rolling boil.

To store: Place cooked meatballs in a single layer on waxed paper. Cover loosely and place in freezer about 2 hours. When frozen, transfer meatballs to a freezer bag and store in freezer.

To serve: Place desired number of frozen soup balls in heated soup; simmer 5 minutes or until heated through.
Yield: 30-36 mini-meatballs.

Tofu Fruit Pudding

This recipe packs protein into a lunch-time dessert.

½ cup	tofu (water packed)	125 mL
½ cup	soft peaches, nectarines or applesauce	125 mL
4 drops	vanilla	4 drops
	Sugar, brown sugar or honey, if necessary	
Pinch	cinnamon, optional	Pinch

Drain tofu and place in a clean cloth, twist cloth closed and squeeze or knead tofu for 2-3 minutes, being careful not to press so hard that the tofu begins to come through. In a blender or food processor, purée tofu, fruit and vanilla. If necessary sweeten with sugar or honey; stir in cinnamon, if desired. Chill about 30 minutes.

NOTE: When you're adding sweetener, remember your child isn't used to foods as sweet as you may like, so keep the amount of sugar added to a minimum.
Yield: Two ⅓-cup (75-mL) servings.

The Overweight Toddler

Forget what you've heard about fat babies being destined to become fat teens and adults. It needn't apply. In fact, parents often mistake a big toddler for an overweight one and dangerously restrict his diet. A protruding stomach and a round face doesn't mean your child is too fat. Look instead for excess rolls of fat in the upper arms and thighs.

Obesity, however, does seem to run in families. The reasons are many — inherited body shape, the habits and attitudes to food learned at home and the importance placed on physical activity. Examine the way you are presenting food. Toddlers should not be praised for eating, nor should they be reprimanded when they don't eat. Giving cookies or ice cream as a reward or for consolation may start a habit of turning to food as a way of coping with frustration.

Think of a chubby toddler as being too short for his weight. He doesn't need to lose pounds, just not gain as much as he grows taller.

Fat is twice as loaded with calories as protein or carbohydrates, so some ways you can reduce energy (caloric) intake, but not mealtime bulk are:

- Spread the butter or margarine thinner on toast, and leave it out of sandwiches altogether.
- Serve your child skim milk — it is safe to do so after he is two years old.
- Use cottage cheese or low-fat cheese.
- Trim all visible fat from meat before serving.
- Use chicken (no skin) and fish more often than the fattier cured meats such as bologna and wieners.
- Cook by roasting, baking or poaching, rather than frying.

Special reduced-fat foods, such as low-fat cheese, ice cream or yogurt, are fine for children over the age of two. It is also safe to use sugar-reduced, calorie-free foods, such as diet pop, as extras (see page 116). However, such foods should not take the place of needed servings of fruit, juice or milk.

For most children it's not necessary to limit the number of servings of bread, cereals, vegetables and fruit at mealtimes. More than likely it's the between-meal snacks that are out of hand. Is your child asking for food because he's bored, or wants attention? Are eating and watching TV taking the place of other activities that would burn up calories?

Children don't like to be told to exercise, but they do like to play with their friends and with their parents. Playing tag, throwing balls, riding a tricycle, climbing and sliding on playground equipment are all great ways for young children to develop coordination and muscle strength, burn off calories and become fit.

Become involved in your child's activities. Play hide-and-seek around the house, put on some music and dance together, toss a ball or a frisbee, take a walk around the neighbourhood and pick up cans or other recyclables, visit the local swimming pool or fly a kite in the park. The whole family will benefit with better health and closer relationships.

7

NO BECOMES A FAVORITE WORD
Three-Year-Olds

Kathy was saying her prayers: "Dear God, thank you for Mommy and Daddy and baby Paul. Thank you for my swing set, and my doll ...
"Mommy, do I thank God for liver?"
"You can if you want to dear," replied mom, stifling a smile.
"Dear God, thank you for ..." After a long pause, Kathy sadly turned to her mom. "Mommy, I just can't thank God for liver. Do I have to? I hate liver."

Can you celebrate "No"? For a two- or three-year-old toddler, it is a milestone. Your child is demonstrating his ability to think independently. It's likely he's using one of your favorite words to him.

For the next dozen years or more you will be challenged teaching him to modify his *noes* to a more socially acceptable form and frequency. You'll want him to learn to accommodate the wishes of others, especially yours, without losing his spirit.

At this stage, probably the easiest way to foster independent thinking while still maintaining control, is to offer choices. To use the corporate buzz terminology, avoid win-lose by creating win-win situations. Would you like a banana or an orange for dessert? Do you want your milk in your cup or in a glass? Do you want your meat or your vegetables first? (It doesn't really matter what order the food goes into his stomach.)

Of course that strategy alone won't guarantee easy mealtimes with toddlers. Nothing works all the time. As parents, you need plenty of patience and a sense of humor at this stage. You'll be coping with picky appetites, food fixations, food jags and eating rituals. There will be days when it seems that no matter what you make, someone will say, "I don't like it." When I had three preschoolers it seemed that I could count on at least one "yuck" at every dinner.

Even the way you prepare the food can be wrong. If you normally cut sandwiches in triangles, but one day cut them into rectangles, you're sunk. From then on, no matter which you do, you'll be making the wrong choice unless you first consult your household's supreme authority.

If you like variety in your meals, you can be sure your toddler will be one who gains security from sameness. Expect to go through the yogurt, the cottage cheese, the peanut butter and the spaghetti stages. Fortunately, even if eaten for five out of seven lunches a week, these foods have nutritional benefits.

And take heart. Food jags are generally short-lived. One day, you'll find your refrigerator stocked with processed cheese slices, only to discover they are no longer in vogue.

Being a reasonable and less demanding adult seems to help a child to become more reasonable and less demanding.

Realistic Expectations

Some of the frustrations parents experience at this time can be avoided by viewing the situations from your child's point of view.

He likes his food simple. If you go to a lot of trouble preparing gourmet treats he doesn't like, you're setting yourself up for frustration. Maybe ground beef, chicken and cheese are the mainstays of his diet now, but he's not suffering nutritionally. You can still cook ratatouille for you and your mate. Chances are, he'll become suspicious if he sees you enjoying something different and want a taste. Let him try a little of your "grown-up food," and if he likes it, promise to cook a portion for him next time.

If food is used as a bribe, expect behavior designed to earn the reward. If your child is promised ice cream if she'll stop crying, even when ice cream is not the dessert choice that day, you can expect a temper tantrum another day. She's learned to manipulate you with her fussing.

It's natural to be suspicious of "it's good for you" foods. None of us likes to be told what we should and should not do. And because green beans have iron is not a reason to like the taste. But food presented matter-of-factly is much easier to tolerate.

There's no nutritional reason to deny your child a fruit dessert just because he didn't finish his carrots. Apricots and carrots provide many of the same essential vitamins. But if he wants a second serving of French toast, you can require him to eat some carrots first. In some families, the guideline "one piece for each year," works well. That means a three-year-old only has to finish three pieces of beans; the five-year-old must have five.

Children like to imitate their parents. If chips and beer are part of your TV-watching routine, your child will expect treats with "Mr. Rogers." You need to clean up your own eating habits before you can expect your child to have good eating habits.

Mealtime Routine

"Never say never" means your family's eating pattern and meals aren't based on a lot of rules. But if you have consistent expectations and a daily routine, your children will be able to distinguish and adapt to exceptions.

Some of the routines that work in other families are:

- Relaxed, unhurried meals. If there's a scheduled event at 6:30 P.M., let the toddlers start early. On the other hand, it's too much to expect a three-year-old to be able to sit still while you enjoy your second cup of coffee. Let them leave the table and play, even between courses, and return when you're ready to serve a new food.

- Quiet time, even "Sesame Street" on TV, before a meal sets a more relaxed pace. Handwashing can be done fifteen or twenty minutes before the meal, and be the activity that changes the pace. Toddlers have difficulty eating when they're tired or overexcited.

- Mealtimes are times for sharing the happy experiences of the day. A friend of mine was an expert at turning a dreary day and a dinner of leftovers into a special occasion. All it took was eating in the dining room by candlelight, some festive placemats and her own enthusiasm. Leave the listing of problems and complaints, and the handing out of punishments, to another time.

- Limit eating to sitting down at the table. You will have a better idea of how much is eaten and how much wasted. Some families restrict meals to the kitchen or dining room table to save the living room or family room furniture and carpets. Others don't mind snacks in the family room, but insist that their children sit down, with placemats, on the floor.

Support Each Other

Support, encouragement and plenty of words of praise and thanks for the meals are more than polite manners. They are essential for the cook's morale. It's too much to expect sincere thank yous from your toddlers with any regularity, but perhaps your partner can set an example and praise the meal in their presence. You mightn't think the children notice, but habits built slowly stick for a long time.

Solutions to Common Complaints

Mealtime is so messy. Children like to experiment with their food — the textures are such fun. If you can't tolerate the stirring and mixing and the finger eating at the family dinner table, let your child eat ahead. He'll soon learn that family eating offers other rewards that he may want. Then he may be ready to restrict his food experiments to lunch time, or to the times when he helps you cook.

He refuses all vegetables. First of all, while vegetables are important sources of many essential vitamins and minerals, fruits also contain many of the same nutrients and can be a good alternative much of the time. (For more on these nutrients, see Chapter Fifteen.)

But more important, vegetables should be more than a duty food. Vegetable preparation deserves the same thought and care in preparation as meat dishes. Keep the flavor fresh and the color bright, by not overcooking. Overcooking robs the vegetable of its inherent good flavor. When cooking dark green vegetables such as spinach, broccoli, Brussels sprouts and green beans, leave the cover off. During cooking, these vegetables release organic acids, which, if trapped, can change the color to a dull, olive green and can make the taste almost unpalatable.

Vegetable Variations

- Introduce turnips or rutabaga by cutting in small cubes and cooking in a vegetable or meat and vegetable soup.
- Cooked turnips or beets are good shredded and sautéed in butter.
- Sweet potatoes are excellent baked in their skins and served with butter. Or, substitute sweet potatoes or yams in a favorite recipe for Twice-Baked Potatoes.
- Easy Cheese Sauce: Lay processed cheese slices over hot steamed or microwaved vegetables; cover and allow to steam about 30-60 seconds. This addition certainly turns kids onto vegetables like broccoli, cauliflower, etc.
- Cabbage is great in cabbage rolls, stuffed with a meat mixture; or cooked, herbed beans; or even a tomato-rice mixture. But it's also good sautéed in butter with a few sliced apples added just after the cabbage is tender. To add color to meals, try this idea with red cabbage: sprinkle it with a few drops of vinegar or lemon juice, just before serving.
- Halved, hollowed and lightly steamed zucchini make great "boats" for meat or vegetable mixtures; bake and serve topped with tomato sauce and melted mozzarella cheese.
- Purée cooked parsnips or sweet potatoes with a peeled and cored ripe pear; add a few drops of lemon juice; heat and serve.
- Serve steamed Brussels sprouts or cabbage tossed in plain yogurt and garnished with grated Parmesan cheese.
- Frozen peas are brightened when cooked with some cubed red pepper, chopped celery and onion.
- Nutmeg and cinnamon are excellent condiments to use

with yellow vegetables such as carrots, squash and sweet potatoes.

- A squeeze of fresh lemon juice decreases or eliminates the need for salt on steamed fresh vegetables.
- Sweeten vegetables with a little fruit — pears with parsnips, apples with squash.
- Fresh green peas and beans, and cherry tomatoes taste extra special when eaten right from the garden. A backyard plot is an ideal way to foster interest in vegetables. If you haven't the room, you can grow window pots of parsley and herbs that your child can pick and add to the vegetables.

Cheesy Vegetable Casserole

1½ cups	fresh broccoli, cut into bite-sized pieces	375 mL
1½ cups	fresh cauliflower, cut into flowerets	375 mL
1 cup	thinly sliced carrots	250 mL
2 tbsp	butter or margarine	25 mL
3 tbsp	flour	45 mL
1 cup	milk	250 mL
½ tsp	salt	1 mL
⅛ tsp	pepper	0.5 mL
Pinch	nutmeg	Pinch
¾ cup	grated Cheddar cheese, divided	175 mL

Heat oven to 400°F (200°C). Cook vegetables in small amount of boiling water until tender, about 5-7 minutes. Drain well. Melt butter, add flour and cook for 30 seconds. Gradually stir in milk and bring to a boil, stirring constantly. Cook for 1 minute. Remove from heat. Add salt, pepper, nutmeg and ½ cup (125 mL) cheese; blend. Spoon vegetables into a 4-cup (1-L) casserole dish. Pour sauce over and top with remaining cheese. Bake at 400°F (200°C) for about 20 minutes or until bubbly.

Yield: four ½-cup (125-mL) servings.

Some children don't like food mixtures; others will readily eat vegetables in soups or casseroles. If your children like soup, it becomes an easy way to serve vegetables at noon time.

Creamy Cauliflower Soup

1	small head cauliflower	1
1	10-oz/284-mL can chicken broth	1
½ cup	instant non-fat dry milk powder	125 mL
2½ cups	milk	625 mL
2 tbsp	butter or margarine	25 mL
2 tbsp	all-purpose flour	25 mL
¼ tsp	dried oregano	1 mL
½ tsp	freshly ground pepper	2 mL
⅓ cup	plain yogurt	75 mL

Remove leaves and wash cauliflower; separate flowerets and chop coarsely. Combine cauliflower and chicken broth in a large saucepan. Cover and bring to a boil. Reduce heat and simmer 5-8 minutes, just until cauliflower is tender. Cool slightly. Purée in blender or food processor until smooth; set aside.

   Add milk powder to milk, stirring until dissolved. Rinse saucepan and melt butter in it. Add flour and oregano; stir over medium heat 2 minutes. Slowly add milk, stirring constantly. Continue cooking, stirring occasionally, until mixture thickens slightly. Stir in puréed cauliflower and pepper; simmer, DO NOT BOIL, 5 minutes. Just before serving, stir in yogurt and adjust seasoning to taste.

Yield: about 7 cups (1.5 L).

Creamy Broccoli Soup: Steam broccoli flowerets as a vegetable side dish or use flowerets as appetizers in a tasty dip. Peel and chop the stems for soup. Substitute 1 bunch broccoli or 3-4 cups (750 mL-1 L) peeled, coarsely chopped broccoli stems for cauliflower in above recipe.

Many vegetables — turnips and cauliflower, for example — have a milder taste when eaten raw. Offer your hungry bunnies raw vegetables with a simple yogurt or cottage cheese dip (or just some French dressing) as a before-dinner snack. Then they won't have to eat any vegetables at mealtime.

Cheesy Yogurt Dip

½ cup	cream cheese, softened	125 mL
2-3 tbsp	plain yogurt	25-45 mL
2 tbsp	finely chopped green onions	25 mL
1 tbsp	finely chopped parsley	15 mL
¼ tsp	salt	1 mL
Dash	pepper	Dash
2 drops	Worcestershire sauce	2 drops

Beat cream cheese with yogurt until smooth. Add remaining ingredients and blend well. Serve with cut-up pieces of fresh vegetables.
Yield: about ¾ cup (200 mL) dip.

The next dip can be used for vegetables or crackers, as a stuffing for celery sticks or as a spread on sandwiches.

Cheesy Lentil Dip

¾ cup	cooked lentils, drained or	175 mL
½ can	19-oz/540-mL can lentils, drained	½ can
⅓ cup	cream cheese (2 oz/57 g), cut into cubes	50 mL
2-3 tsp	taco sauce or spaghetti sauce	10-15 mL

Combine lentils, cream cheese and taco sauce in container of blender or food processor. Purée until smooth. Serve with vegetable sticks, bread sticks, crackers, etc.

TIP: Use chopped onion, herbs, hot pepper sauce or dry soup mixes with or instead of taco sauce to season this dip.

Yield: 1 cup (250 mL) dip.

Vegetable Fingers

4	medium parsnips	4
	All-purpose flour	
⅓ cup	evaporated milk	75 mL
1 cup	Oven Coating (recipe follows)	250 mL

Peel parsnips and cut each in half. Cut bottom half lengthwise into 2 pieces; top part into 4 pieces. Steam parsnips over boiling water 6-10 minutes or just until tender. Cool slightly.

Coat parsnip fingers with flour; dip in evaporated milk and then roll in Oven Coating. If desired, dip in evaporated milk and Oven Coating a second time to assure a thorough covering. Place on a greased baking sheet leaving ample space between fingers. Bake in a 400°F (200°C) oven 15-20 minutes, turning at least twice, until golden brown.

TIP: Vegetable Fingers can also be made with carrots or peeled broccoli stems. Be sure to cut vegetables into a uniform size

and steam just until tender. Coated vegetables can also be frozen and baked later.
Yield: 24 fingers.

Oven Coating

¾ cup	dry bread crumbs	175 mL
¼ cup	grated Parmesan cheese	50 mL
Pinch	dried thyme or oregano, optional	Pinch

Combine crumbs, cheese and thyme if desired. Store in a tightly covered container in refrigerator.
Yield: 1 cup (250 mL).

She just doesn't seem to enjoy her meals. If your child frequently rejects your planned meals, you're going to have to decide whether to allow substitutes or not. Are her requests for alternatives nutritious and easy to prepare — a peanut butter sandwich, yogurt or fruit instead of vegetables? If they are, giving in will make mealtime more enjoyable for everyone. Is she being difficult to get attention? That may be a sign your meal preparation may have lost its creativity.

A little flair and imagination can go a long way with children. Add a few treats:

- a fresh strawberry at the bottom of the custard
- banana slices in the pancakes
- apple chunks on top of the cereal
- sandwiches in the shape of animals (use a cookie cutter)

Dietitian Carolyn Clark uses the element of surprise to tempt little ones on the not-too-hungry days. A favorite lunch in her house is Cheese Meltie Surprise.

Cheese Meltie Surprise

1	slice whole wheat toast, buttered	1
1	pineapple ring, drained	1
1	slice, processed cheese or	1
1 oz	grated Cheddar cheese	30 g

Place pineapple ring on toast and top with cheese. Put under broiler until cheese bubbles. (Alternatively, cook in the microwave for 30 seconds.)

NOTE: Instead of pineapple, other surprises to use under the cheese are: tomato slice (sprinkled with basil for gourmet kids), olives, sliced mushrooms or all of the above. If you substitute mozzarella cheese for the Cheddar, you have pizza on toast.

Yield: 1 serving.

Kellogg knew what they were doing when they put snap, crackle and pop into Rice Krispies. Children enjoy variety in texture and sound, as well as taste. Combine crisp, chewy, soft and smooth in one meal. In a fruit cocktail you can combine crispy apple wedges, tart grapefruit sections, and soft and mild banana slices. If your child is allowed to pick out the cherries — and you eat them instead — chances are next time she'll eat all the fruits.

A Word about Sweets

A frequent question is, "Should children have dessert if they haven't finished their vegetables?" I think one serving of dessert is fine. It doesn't become a big issue if dessert has nutritional value — yogurt, milk pudding, fruit, apple crisp, oatmeal cookies.

Most people have a sweet tooth — they enjoy the flavor of

sweeter foods. Even newborn babies can distinguish between plain and sweetened water; they'll suck longer on the sugar solutions. But for many children sweets have an added emotional appeal. The giving of sweets becomes intertwined with the giving of love or rewards.

Other parents feel guilty about the sweets their children are eating. They make a major production out of banning them from the house, and that just adds to their charm as a forbidden treat.

A few years ago Dr. Lewis A. Coffin wrote a book, *The Grandmother Conspiracy Exposed*. Much of the advice in his book is very sensible. However, one of Dr. Coffin's pet peeves is the amount of sugar children eat. He refers to sugar as a slow poison. I think that's overreacting.

Many good foods, such as milk and fruit, naturally contain sugar. It's not that natural sugar is better than the sucrose in our sugar bowl; it's just that these foods also contain other essential nutrients, and the amount of sugar is not out of proportion. For a three-year-old an oatmeal cookie, an ice cream dessert or a sweetened pudding can also be part of the menu. After all, these foods provide important nutrients as well.

How then should parents handle sweets — the kind that have few additional nutrients? Moderation is the key, as it is with all foods. Accept that sweet foods are ingrained in our social pattern. Chocolates at Valentine's Day and Easter, cake on your birthday, candies at Halloween and as thank yous are as much a part of our eating rituals as turkey at Thanksgiving and goose at Christmas. However, special occasion foods lose their "uniqueness" if they become everyday. So enjoy the treats with your children on occasion, without feeling guilty.

But realize that children have difficulty understanding that candies are just tokens of love — not the real thing. If every grazed knee, hurt feeling or grandmother's visit involves sweet treats, he'll expect the candy — not the hug — as a symbol you care. He may even come to expect sweets as just payment for every nasty situation, such as an innoculation.

You don't offer an apple to take away the hurt of an insect bite. Similarly, if you can keep the emotions out of sweets, and just acknowledge them for what they are — good tastes — you'll be on the road to a reasonable, balanced approach. Children love the taste of hot dogs, but they rarely throw temper tantrums over hot dogs. That's because there is no emotion mixed up with the giving of hot dogs.

Sugar Substitutes

Sugar substitutes and high-intensity sweeteners, such as aspartame (NutraSweet), won't hurt your child. In fact, sugar-free gum, yogurt, ice cream and other foods can be a godsend for children with diabetes, weight problems or dental disease. But most young children need the energy from sugar, along with the vitamins and other nutrients in fruit, juice or milk. In fact, when schoolchildren were given diet pop instead of a sugar-containing beverage at recess, they had more difficulty sitting still and studying. It wasn't that aspartame caused restlessness, but rather that hungry children can't concentrate as well.

Note: Diabetic children can have some sugar-containing foods. Talk to a professional dietitian to find out how much and when it would be appropriate.

When a Sweet Dessert Is Appropriate

Soft Oatmeal Raisin Cookies

¾ cup	whole wheat flour	175 mL
¾ cup	all-purpose flour	175 mL
1 tsp	salt	5 mL
¾ tsp	baking soda	4 mL
1 tsp	cinnamon	5 mL

¾ cup	butter or margarine	175 mL
¾ cup	brown sugar	175 mL
2	eggs	2
⅓ cup	milk	75 mL
1½ cups	rolled oats	375 mL
2 cups	raisins	500 mL
	or	
1 cup	raisins	250 mL
	and	
1 cup	cut-up, dried apricots	250 mL
½ cup	chopped nuts, optional	125 mL

Heat oven to 375°F (190°C). Combine flours, salt, baking soda and cinnamon. In large mixer bowl, cream butter, sugar and eggs together until light and fluffy. Add flour mixture alternately with milk. Stir in oats, raisins and nuts, if desired. Drop by tablespoons on lightly greased cookie sheets. Bake at 375°F (190°C) 10-12 minutes or until golden. Cool sheets on wire racks 5 minutes before removing cookies.
Yield: about 4 dozen cookies.

For birthday parties, Cone Cakes are easier to handle than regular cake. Let the youngsters help in the baking and/or decorating. Place a name tag in each Cone Cake; youngsters love making special ones for each friend.

Cone Cakes

Flat-bottom ice cream cones
Moist cake or muffin batter
Buttercream or fluffy icing
Cake decorator sprinkles or finely chopped nuts, raisins or gum drops

Stand ice cream cones in muffin cups. Spoon cake or muffin

batter into cones, filling ⅔ full. (Use any remaining cake batter for a layer cake or regular cup cakes.)

Bake according to cake mix or recipe directions for cup cakes. (Baking time will be somewhat shorter than that specified for normal muffins.) Cake will rise up forming a slight peak on cone. Cool completely.

If using buttercream icing, whip thoroughly with a little extra cream or milk until icing holds a soft peak. Place icing in a small, deep bowl. Holding cone, dip and turn in icing until coated. Coat with cake decorator sprinkles.

8

CHOICES IN THE GROCERY STORE

The best meals are built around plenty of fresh foods — lean meats, fish, poultry, milk and dairy products, fruits and vegetables — prepared lovingly at home. But in busy families, where time and energy for shopping and cooking is often at a premium, convenience foods become a necessity. And if carefully chosen, they will not jeopardize the nutritional balance of family meals or the health of your preschooler.

---

*I remember one shopping trip with my preschoolers when I was feeling very harassed. They started their ·
why routine: "Why can't we have Happy Time cereal?"
In my frustration I found myself answering, in my best lecturing voice, "Because I'm a nutritionist."*

There certainly are better reasons for choosing or not choosing certain prepackaged foods. I hope the advice below will help you make your choices rationally.

119

Breakfast Foods

Fruit juices or drinks

Juices are extracted from real fruits; fruit drinks are primarily artificially produced beverages consisting of flavor extracts, sugar, colorings and water. Many fruit drinks also have added vitamin C, and certain brands contain some fruit juice, maybe ten percent. Thus both juices and drinks can be a good source of energy and vitamin C.

But juices provide more — minerals such as potassium, and other vitamins such as folic acid. Unsweetened fruit juices have slightly less sugar than drinks, sweetened fruit juices as much or more.

For flavor and extra nutrition, I prefer unsweetened juices (fresh, frozen or canned). But families who choose fruit drinks for economic reasons are also serving a source of vitamin C if they choose a vitamin-enriched product and if they practice careful preparation and storage. Vitamin C in fruits, vegetables, juices and drinks is easily destroyed during exposure to air or heat. Refrigerated, covered storage of reconstituted drinks or juices is necessary to retain vitamin value. Even then, significant losses occur in just twenty-four hours. Because juices are generally acidic, the rate of vitamin loss is less than with fruit drinks.

Breakfast Cereals

Many families find ready-to-eat cereals a convenient breakfast choice. Served with milk, cereals are also a nutritious choice.

Health professionals have rediscovered the health benefits of fiber (or old-fashioned bulk) in our diets, so our preference is for whole grain or bran-containing cereals. You'll have a number of choices; just read the labels. Similarly, whole grain cooked cereals — even the instant cooking varieties — are an excellent choice.

Many cereals have added vitamins and iron to increase their nutritional value. But remember, the iron content of family-type cereals is not as high as the iron content of infant cereals. Keep your baby on the infant cereals until he's well over the age of one and eating meat, egg yolk or legumes daily.

One of the biggest areas of concern for dietitians and nutritionists is sugar-coated cereals. Certainly children rarely need extra sugar, and ideally you shouldn't start the habit of sprinkling sugar (or honey or molasses) on cereal. Also, if children snack on sugar-coated cereals between meals, they are more likely to develop cavities. All dry cereals easily become stuck between the teeth, providing an ideal breeding ground for decay-causing bacteria.

But what about sugar-coated cereals at breakfast, when the milk on the cereal will help wash away the sugar, and you are more likely to clean your child's teeth? Some cereal manufacturers argue that the amount of sugar they add to cereal is less than the amount many parents add. (A teaspoon of sugar is about five grams of sugar.) So if the sugar bowl is on your table, the argument against sugar-coated cereals is not as strong. If you do serve your children a sugar-coated cereal, be sure they don't add even more sugar.

Granola

Granola sounds like a perfect cereal for older children who don't mind chewing — full of fiber-rich grains and protein-rich nuts. But commercial granola is also very high in fat, as well as sugar from the added honey and molasses. For a healthier granola, make a batch from the recipe that follows. I've adapted it so that it has the minimum added sweetener.

Granola

4 cups	rolled oats	1 L
1 cup	skim milk powder	250 mL
½ cup	wheat germ	125 mL
½ cup	wheat bran	125 mL
½ cup	chopped nuts	125 mL
¼ cup	coconut	50 mL
½ cup	sunflower kernels	125 mL
¼ cup	sesame seeds	50 mL
⅓ cup	liquid honey	75 mL
½ cup	corn oil	125 mL
	Raisins or dried fruit, optional	

In a large bowl mix dry ingredients well. Add honey and corn oil, and continue to stir until all the dry ingredients are coated. Spread out in a casserole and bake in a 350°F (180°C) oven for 20-30 minutes, or until golden brown. Stir once or twice during baking for even brownness.

Microwave: In a large microwave-safe bowl, mix ingredients as above. Microwave at LOW (30%) for 6 minutes, stir and microwave for 6 minutes twice more. Store in a closed container. *Yield:* twenty-one ⅓-cup (75-mL) servings.

Eggs

Eggs have taken a beating lately. The discovery of the link between heart disease and cholesterol has meant that many people have cut back on their use of eggs. Certainly eggs contain more cholesterol than most other foods, and adults who have high blood cholesterol (the majority) do need to moderate their intake. For adults, two to five eggs per week is about right, depending upon the amount of exercise you get and your blood fat values.

But most young children don't have high blood cholesterol values. (There are some exceptions.) And they do need a certain amount of cholesterol for brain and nerve growth. Because eggs have other nutritional benefits — particularly iron and protein — I believe five to seven eggs a week is not too many for young children.

What children do not need is eggs fried in large amounts of bacon fat, butter, margarine or oil. Most of the time, serve them scrambled in a minimum of fat or poached or baked. They can also be added to pudding, meatloaf, etc.

For a fun way to combine the egg and cereal courses, try the following recipe from General Foods.

Eggs in Cereal Nests

3 tbsp	butter or margarine, melted	45 mL
2 cups	bran flakes	500 mL
1 cup	Cheddar cheese, grated	250 mL
4	eggs	4
	Salt and pepper, to taste	

Melt butter in oven, and combine with bran flakes and cheese. Spread cereal mixture over the bottom of 4 individual baking dishes, making a depression or "nest" in the center of each one. Break 1 egg into each nest. Sprinkle with salt and pepper. Bake at 425°F (220°C) 10-12 minutes, or until eggs reach desired doneness.

Microwave: Assemble as above. Microwave on HIGH (100%) for 2 minutes.

Yield: 4 servings.

Breads and Baked Goods

My preference is for whole grain breads, for the extra fiber. But enriched white bread is still a good food. Iron and the B vitamins — thiamin, riboflavin and niacin — that were lost in milling are replaced. Whole wheat bread has more of another B vitamin, folic acid.

Introduce your children to a variety of breads — white, whole wheat, rye, cracked wheat and pumpernickel. Chances are they'll enjoy many of them. More often it's what's on the bread that's important to a child, not the kind of bread.

As well, use other nutritious baked goods made with whole grain or enriched flours — muffins, rolls, English muffins, bagels, crumpets, scones. Save baked products that are especially high in fat and sugar — doughnuts, croissants, cakes, Danish pastries and pies — for occasional use only.

Lunch and Dinner Foods

We covered many favorite lunch-time foods above, but what about others?

Bacon and Cured Meats

Cured meats such as bacon, ham, bologna, salami and wieners have added sodium. And high intakes of sodium (salt — sodium chloride — and other sodium compounds) throughout life are associated with a greater risk of high blood pressure. Many cured meats are also high in fat. Therefore, although they're very convenient to use, I recommend you limit your use of cured meats to one or two servings a week.

One thing you may have read about cured meats is that they contain nitrite, and that nitrite and nitrate are associated with cancer. That's true, but the amount of nitrite permitted in Canadian meats is small — just enough to prevent a more serious risk, botulism poisoning. As well, today's cured meats contain either ascorbate (vitamin C) or erythorbate (a non-vitamin). These two compounds cause nitrites to be converted rapidly to color pigments in the meat, thereby virtually eliminating the amount of nitrite left behind. Less nitrite means less potentially harmful carcinogens.

Canned Tuna and Salmon

They're great. You can remove most of the oil added in canning by rinsing in cold water. You can also buy water-packed canned fish, but it's usually more expensive.

Cheeses, Yogurt and Other Dairy Products

Practically all dairy products are important sources of calcium and protein. The exception is ice cream, which doesn't provide much protein. Introduce your children to a wide variety of cheeses — Canadian Cheddar, Danish Danbo and Havarti, Dutch Gouda, Swiss Gruyère. Who knows, you may have a Danish Blue fan in your house.

Processed cheese spread or slices are handy to use and often a childhood favorite. Generally speaking, processed cheeses are lower in calcium, fat and protein, and much higher in sodium and moisture than natural (unprocessed) cheese.

Although included in this lunch-time section, cheese also makes an excellent breakfast food or snack. It seems to help protect teeth from decay.

Pasta Products

Noodles and spaghetti provide starch, a complex carbohydrate that's an important energy source for children. There is such a versatility of sauces you can use — vegetable, meat, cheese — that you needn't be concerned if pasta products become a major item in your child's menus. For maximum nutritional value, choose pasta products that have added B vitamins and iron. You'll see the word "enriched" on the label.

Canned or packaged pasta mixes won't have as much protein, or flavor, as your own homemade toppings. But if meat is being served at another meal that day, there's no harm in using these convenience foods, especially if you don't relish macaroni and cheese five days a week, but your child does. If packaged macaroni and cheese is a favorite in your household, follow the package directions, and then add variety with the following ideas.

Macaroni and Cheese Dress-Ups

1. Double Cheese: Stir ½ cup (125 mL) cottage cheese, or cubed processed cheese, or ⅓ cup (75 mL) grated Cheddar or mozzarella cheese, into hot Macaroni and Cheese.
2. Drizzle each serving of Macaroni and Cheese with Spaghetti Meat Sauce.
3. Brown ¼ lb (125 g) ground meat — beef, pork, lamb — drain thoroughly and stir into Macaroni and Cheese.
4. Stir ½ cup (125 mL) drained, seeded and chopped fresh or canned tomatoes into hot Macaroni and Cheese.
5. Baked Specialty: Combine additions 3 and 4 with Macaroni and Cheese; turn into a greased casserole and top with buttered bread crumbs. Bake in a 350°F (180°C) oven 10-15 minutes until golden brown and bubbly around edges.
6. Pasta Fazule: Stir 1 cup (250 mL) cooked, heated kidney beans and a pinch of dried oregano or thyme into hot prepared Macaroni and Cheese. Top each serving with grated Parmesan, Cheddar or mozzarella cheese.
7. Macaroni and Cheese with Flowers: Steam 1 cup small broccoli or cauliflower flowerets just until tender. Toss lightly with hot Macaroni and Cheese; serve immediately.
8. Chic Macaroni and Cheese: Cut 4 oz (125 g) boneless chicken or turkey into small strips or cubes. In a skillet, heat oil with ½ chopped onion or 1 clove garlic. Sauté chicken until golden. Toss with hot, prepared Macaroni and Cheese.
9. Wieneriffic Macaroni and Cheese: Slice 2-3 wieners into coins, heat and toss with hot prepared Macaroni and Cheese.
10. Ham Julienne: Toss hot prepared Macaroni and Cheese with cooked ham cut into julienne pieces.

11. Vegetable Julienne: Cut carrot, celery, onion or a mixture of other vegetables into julienne strips. Steam or sauté until tender. Toss with hot prepared Macaroni and Cheese.
12. Harvest Bake: Add a can of tuna, drained and flaked, chopped tomatoes and ¼ cup (50 mL) milk to Macaroni and Cheese. Top with grated Parmesan cheese and bake at 350°F (180°C) for 20 minutes.

Hot Pasta Salad

Hot Pasta Salad is a good make-ahead dish — prepare as directed, using whatever shape noodles you prefer, and store in refrigerator. At mealtime reheat in microwave or oven.

2	carrots, scraped	2
2	stalks celery including leaves, cleaned	2
½ cup	chicken broth or water	125 mL
½ cup	frozen peas	125 mL
4 cups	cooked spiral pasta or macaroni	1 L
2 oz	mozzarella cheese, cut into small cubes	60 g
1 cup	cottage cheese	250 mL
¾ cup	spaghetti sauce	175 mL
2 tbsp	grated Parmesan cheese, optional	25 mL

Cut carrots and celery into ¼-in. (6-mm) cubes and simmer in chicken broth over medium heat until almost tender. Add peas and continue cooking until all vegetables are softened. Drain, reserving cooking liquid. In a large bowl, combine vegetables, cooked pasta, and mozzarella and cottage cheeses; toss thoroughly and turn into a 10-cup (1.5-L) greased casserole. Combine reserved vegetable cooking liquid and spaghetti sauce; pour over pasta mixture. Cover and bake in a 350°F (180°C) oven 25 minutes. Uncover, sprinkle with Parmesan cheese; continue baking 10 minutes or until heated through.

Microwave: Decrease broth to ¼ cup (50 mL) and place in microwave dish with carrots and celery. Cover and microwave on HIGH (100%) 4 minutes. Stir in peas; cover dish and microwave on HIGH 4 minutes; let stand 3 minutes. Drain, reserving cooking liquid. Combine ingredients as above. Cover and microwave on HIGH 4 minutes; then microwave at MEDIUM (50%) 15 minutes or until heated through. Carefully remove plastic wrap and sprinkle with Parmesan cheese. Cover and let stand for 5-10 minutes.

Yield: six 1-cup (250-mL) servings.

Pizza and Tacos

The wonderful thing about pizzas and tacos is that they can have so many different tastes. Even if you buy ready-to-serve, you can add extra nutrition with more toppings. Both are wonderful ways to disguise the less popular vegetables.

Soups

Canned soups, particularly the vegetable-based soups, retain many of the nutrients from the original vegetables, although soups are high in salt. Dried soups are less nutritious; much of the vitamin goodness is lost during processing.

When you're using soups, consider adding your own left-overs — vegetables or meats — to vary the flavor. Also try the convenient Soup Ball recipe from Chapter Six.

Frozen Dinners

Although some frozen dinners are too salty for a young child, others are fine. (The ones that are lowest in salt usually advertise that fact on the label.) Some have too much fat — battered fish and chips, for example — but others use lean products. Generally, from an adult's point of view, the problem with frozen TV dinners is their bland flavor, but that may be the reason for their appeal to young children.

From an economic point of view, frozen dinners don't make much sense. However, if you want a night off from cooking, especially when you'll be eating out and the children will be left with a sitter, go ahead and indulge.

Fish Sticks

Frozen fish sticks are a very convenient food, but you'll be paying fish prices for the batter. It's just as easy to cook fish fillets, without the batter and all that extra fat.

Scalloped Fish and Potato

3	large potatoes, cooked and sliced	3
3	green onions, finely sliced	3
1 lb	fish fillets	500 g
½ tsp	thyme	2 mL
½ tsp	salt, divided	2 mL
¼ tsp	pepper, divided	1 mL
3 tbsp	butter or margarine	45 mL
3 tbsp	flour	45 mL
1½ cups milk		375 mL
½ cup	grated Cheddar cheese	125 mL
¼ tsp	dry mustard	1 mL

Heat oven to 400°F (200°C). Layer sliced potatoes in an 11×7-in. (28×17-cm) baking dish. Sprinkle with green onions and top with fish in single layer. Sprinkle with thyme, ¼ tsp (1 mL) salt and ⅛ tsp (0.5 mL) pepper. Melt butter, add flour and cook for 30 seconds. Gradually stir in milk and bring to a boil, stirring constantly. Cook for 1 minute. Remove from heat. Stir in cheese, dry mustard and remaining salt and pepper. Pour over fish. Bake at 400°F (200°C), for 25 minutes or until fish flakes with a fork.

Microwave: Cover and microwave on HIGH (100%) 9-10 minutes. Let stand 5 minutes before serving.

Yield: four 1-cup (250-mL) servings.

Desserts and Treats from the Grocery Store

The grocery store is full of treats that contain more sugar and fat than children need — certainly on a daily basis. For day-to-day use, better desserts would be canned or fresh fruit, yogurt, puddings, muffins, even ice cream.

Milk Drinks

Flavored milk, including chocolate milk, isn't as bad as you might think. It does have extra energy — from sugar and fat — but it has all the goodness of the milk as well. Despite what you may have heard, adding chocolate to milk does not destroy the calcium content.

Some other ideas for flavoring milk are:

1. Unsweetened Flavored Drink Crystals: Using only half as much milk as water specified on the package, stir crystals into a small amount (¼ cup/50 mL) of milk until dissolved; stir in remaining milk. Sweeten to taste with sugar or honey. Note: Citrus flavors require more sweetening than do fruit flavors such as raspberry, grape or strawberry. For a single serving, use about ½ tsp (2 mL) unsweetened crystals to 1 cup (250 mL) milk.

2. Frozen Fruit Juice Concentrates (thawed slightly and un-diluted): Stir concentrate into milk until dissolved and the desired flavor level is reached. This will vary tremendously from child to child. Use your imagination to give each flavored milk an exciting "kid appeal" name — Purple Cow, Randy Raspberry, Orange Orangutan, etc.

3. Sodas: For a dessert use the above flavored milks to pre-

pare sodas — simply add a scoop of ice cream or sherbet of compatible flavor and ideally of contrasting color. Serve with colorful straws.

Soft Drinks

I'm not fond of giving children regular or diet pop on a daily basis. Too many children drink soft drinks in place of milk or juices. Although the diet pop doesn't have sugar, these beverages can overfill a small stomach.

Pop is a great party or special occasion treat. When used in this way, there is no need to use artificially sweetened pop, nor is there any harm in it.

Economical Choices

When you want to save money, start by buying powdered skim milk (non-fat dry milk) once your children are over two years of age and eating a full diet. If you introduce powdered milk at this age, chances are they'll accept it without question, at least until they are well into school. The secret to making powdered milk palatable is to prepare it ahead, follow the proportion directions carefully, mix well, and serve icy cold. If that doesn't work, try mixing equal proportions of store-bought milk and home-reconstituted powdered milk. If you start with homogenized milk and reconstituted skim, you'll end up with two-percent milk.

Butter or Margarine?

Some families prefer butter for taste, some choose soft margarines for health reasons, others look for economical hard margarines. Whichever you use, you'll be getting primarily fat, approximately the same vitamins and minerals (only vitamin A is present in significant quantities), and the same number of calories per teaspoon. The exception is diet margarine which has half the calories per teaspoon.

If choosing a margarine for health reasons, look for one that is low in saturated fat. Although an accumulation of cholesterol in your bloodstream can cause blocked and hardened arteries which lead to heart disease or stroke, the main culprit is not the cholesterol in foods.

Actually, our livers make about eighty percent of the cholesterol that's in our bodies. This body cholesterol is made from saturated fat, the kind of fat that predominates in meat, eggs and dairy products such as butter, cream, whole milk, ice cream and full-fat cheeses. The tropical oils — palm, palm kernel and coconut oil — used in some margarines and packaged foods are also highly saturated.

Using a soft margarine that's low in saturated fat, instead of butter or hard margarine, is one way to reduce the amount of cholesterol your body can make. Check the nutritional labels for one that has less than 1.2 grams of saturated fat per serving.

But if your family prefers the taste of butter, you can make other changes to reduce saturated fat:

- Drink skim milk instead of full-fat milk.
- Switch to lower-fat cheeses and ice cream.
- Buy leaner cuts of meat and trim away all visible fat.
- Cook with oils such as corn, safflower, sunflower or olive oil that are low in saturated fat.
- Use these same oils in salad dressings.

Whatever fats you use, don't overdo it. Although young children need fat calories, once the growth spurts of the early years are over, Canadian children and adults tend to eat too much fat. That excess fat is blamed for our high incidence of obesity, heart disease and even cancer.

9

LEARNING WITH FOODS

At three-and-a-half to four, your child's not a baby anymore. She fills your day with a million questions. Why do beans grow on branches? Why do carrots grow in the ground? Why are you pounding the meat? Why do we have to eat supper? Are the popsicles frozen yet? Why is my banana dirty on the inside?

Capture that curiosity. Encourage her to climb up on a chair and help you. This is the time when a child shows more interest in food preparation than ever. She wants to help stir the batter, peel the carrots, put the muffin cups into the tins, lick the spoon and beaters, and eat the blueberries before they go into the batter.

Cooking provides so many opportunities for children to learn through all the senses as they:

- listen for the water to boil, or the popcorn to pop;
- taste the bitter lemon and the sweet cinnamon;
- feel the bread dough change as you knead it, and notice the difference between raw and cooked turnip;
- see the two yellows of bananas and lemons;
- smell the cookies baking.

It's exciting to observe the chemical and physical changes

in foods — the gelatin thickening, the poached egg turning from clear to white. It's not necessary to understand why, just to enjoy.

During a kitchen science lesson your preschooler can practice counting eggs and decide which is biggest. She can try new words — *zucchini, soufflé, purée*. Mom or Dad can learn about metric measures.

Rolling dough or stirring a pudding exercises big arm muscles; peeling eggs and tearing lettuce develop finger coordination.

Safety is an integral part of cooking: the stove is hot, always use pot holders; knives are sharp and should be used carefully; handles of pots must be turned inward. She'll have a reason to practice cleanliness: we always wash our hands before touching food; we use a clean spoon for tasting; we wash the countertops and cutting board after each use.

But most of all, cooking should be fun — for parents as well as for children. It's a time for socializing, for laughing over failures, for savoring successes.

A dietitian friend, Carolyn Clark, commented, "My daughter and the other children I know always seem to end up with the olives stuck on the end of their five fingers while 'helping' make a salad or pizza. So what if three out of five are eaten before they reach their intended use — at least they are savored on the detour."

Tips when Cooking with Children

- Cooking starts with a trip to the grocery store, for just a few key ingredients — not the week's supplies. Let your child buy one of the ingredients with her own quarter. What fun it is to get *four* pennies change.

- There will be fewer accidents if the countertop isn't crowded. You might find it easier to switch to the kitchen table.
- A one-litre measuring cup with a handle makes a good mixing bowl. Teach your youngster to always keep one hand on that handle when using the electric mixer. The bowl is less likely to land on the floor and tiny fingers will be kept away from the beaters.
- Talk as you go, using the correct word for each action, but don't lecture. And if the adult name for the recipe is boring, have fun creating new names based on favorite heros — Polkaroo Pudding, Miss Piggy's Pie, Curious George Canapés, Garfield Stew, and Bert's Breakfast Muffin.
- Remember, *the more the adult does, the less the child learns.* The recipes in this chapter are written with that in mind.

Carolyn Clark's No-Shell Egg-Cracking Technique

1. Strike the egg against a hard edge, preferably the rim of a small dessert dish.
2. Holding the egg over the dish, put both thumbs into the crack and pull apart. The egg will fall into the dish and the shell will stay in the child's hands.
3. An adult can then check for bits of shell before the egg is added to other ingredients in the recipe.

Freddie Frank

With a knife, cut wieners as shown (see diagram that follows). Use tongs to drop wieners into boiling water. During cooking the arms and legs spread out. Meanwhile, put a slice of pro-cessed cheese on bread. Mom or Dad puts it under the broiler (or in microwave) until the cheese is bubbly. After the wiener is cooked, lay it on the cheese. Then it's time to add eyes and mouth with ketchup, mustard or relish.

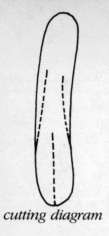

Freddie Frank

cutting diagram *after cooking*

Cheese 'n' Wiener Crescents

1 can	refrigerated crescent roll dough (8 crescents)	1 can
8	wieners	8
8 strips	Cheddar cheese or processed cheese	8 strips

Separate dough into 8 triangles. Slit wieners to within ½ in. (1.5 cm) from ends. Insert a strip of cheese in each wiener. Place on wide end of triangles and roll up. Coat baking sheet with nonstick spray or grease lightly. Place cheese-side-up on baking sheet. Bake at 375°F (190°C) 10-13 minutes or until golden brown. Serve hot.
Yield: 8 sandwiches.

Smile Cookies

1	envelope unflavored gelatin	1
¼ cup	cold fruit juice (orange, raspberry, apple)	50 mL
1 cup	fruit juice, heated just to a boil	250 mL
2 cups	vanilla ice cream, softened	500 mL

> Oatmeal or plain cookies or
> biscuits
> Mandarin orange or orange
> segments or apple or pear
> wedges dipped in lemon juice
> Raisins or chocolate chips
> Peanuts
> Wheat germ or toasted coconut

In a medium bowl, sprinkle unflavored gelatin over cold juice; let stand 1 minute. Add hot juice (parent's task), and stir until gelatin is completely dissolved. With whisk or rotary beater, blend in ice cream. Chill, stirring occasionally, until mixture mounds slightly when dropped from spoon.

Spread mixture on cookies or use mixture as filling for sandwich cookies. Use remaining ingredients to form faces: orange segments for mouth; raisins for eyes; peanuts for noses and eyebrows; wheat germ for hair. Chill until firm.

Turn any remaining mixture into custard cups; chill until set; garnish with any of remaining "face" ingredients.

Yield: determined by size of cookies used.

Whole Grain Pancakes

Making pancakes is a Dad-and-child specialty in our house. Dollar-sized pancakes are ideal for little ones — easier to cut than the larger sizes, if they cut them at all!

Pancake Mix:

1 cup	rolled oats	250 mL
2 tbsp	wheat germ	25 mL
2 tbsp	brown sugar	25 mL
1½ cups	whole wheat flour	375 mL
½ cup	instant non-fat dry milk powder	125 mL
4 tsp	baking powder	20 mL
½ tsp	baking soda	2 mL

Pinch	salt		Pinch

Insert metal blade in food processor or blender. With motor running, pour in oats, wheat germ and sugar. Add flour, milk powder, baking powder, baking soda and salt. Process with an ON/OFF action just until well blended. Mix can be stored in a tightly covered container in a cool place for up to two weeks. *Yield:* 3 batches of mix.

Pancakes:

1	egg	1
1 tbsp	vegetable oil	15 mL
½ cup	milk	125 mL
¼ tsp	vanilla	1 mL
1 cup	Whole Grain Pancake Mix	250 mL

In a large mixing bowl, beat together egg, vegetable oil, milk and vanilla. Stir in pancake mix; let stand at least 5 minutes. Lightly grease a heated griddle. A few drops of water sprinkled on griddle sizzle and bounce when heat is just right. For dollar-sized pancakes use 1 tsp (5 mL) batter for each pancake; for medium pancakes use a scant ¼ cup (50 mL) batter. Pour batter onto hot griddle. Cook until bubbles form and edges start to dry; turn and cook other side.
Yield: 12 medium or 36 dollar-sized pancakes.

Branded Pancakes

Surprise your children with these pancakes. One branded pancake on the top or bottom of a stack of pancakes can help motivate a reluctant eater. They are also ideal for use at a birthday party pancake supper.

This idea works best with slightly thinned, regular buttermilk pancake batter. Whole Grain Pancake batter (above) is not smooth enough for a satisfactory execution.

Pour pancake batter onto heated griddle in shape of child's

initial; wait 2-4 seconds. Top with batter to form pancake. Bake and turn as normal pancake. The initial will brown deeper, "branding" the pancake. Use same technique to make eyes and mouth for "smile" pancakes.

Food for Art

Don't limit food play to just cooking. Some of the best collages are made on plastic meat trays using rice, noodles, cereals and raisins.

Potato Art

Fruits and vegetables — oranges, grapefruit, apples, carrots, onions, green peppers and potatoes — make beautiful prints. Cut the fruits or vegetables in half (either direction). Dry with paper towelling. Then your children can use pencils, plastic spoons, forks or blunt knives to carve a design in the produce.

Make paint pads by folding pieces of paper towelling, about four folds thick, placing the folded paper into separate dishes and saturating the towelling with brightly colored paint. Have children press the fruit lightly on the paint pad. They can use almost any paper for printing.

Potato-printed paper is ideal for gift wrapping or for laminating as a place mat.

Edible Necklaces

As a change from popcorn strings, use Cheerios, Shreddies and a variety of other cereals to make terrific necklaces.

Seed Shakers

Have the child put different seeds and nuts (grapefruit, apple, cherry stones, walnuts, etc.) in empty small juice cans. Glue construction paper over the top, as a cover, and paint and decorate the can. If several children participate, you can have a band!

10

OUT AND ABOUT

Do you need an idea for a family gift? Consider a camp stove, a picnic cooler or plastic dishes. Even if the family isn't into camping, roadside picnics are an ideal way to eat when you're travelling with small children.

Family Camping

I'm partial to camping as the best way to travel with small children. The casual lifestyle is a welcome break from home routine. The children can play and run without your worrying that they are going to bang into furniture or disturb others. They work up a healthy appetite. Spills don't hurt the ground; the squirrels can clean up the crumbs. The cool night air is perfect for sleeping. And it's inexpensive.

Since vacations should be a time of play for everyone, keep meals simple. Experiment with convenience alternatives that are unnecessary and maybe wasteful for home use — canned soups, drinking boxes of juices, variety packs of individual cereal portions, boil-in-bag meals, etc.

For first time family campers, I suggest:

- Safety first. Camp stoves are even more dangerous than

home appliances. Many stove stands are too wobbly or too low to use if you have small children. Instead, put your stove on the picnic table, preferably on a raised box, so it's harder for little hands to touch.

- Use placemats instead of a tablecloth so the spills can slip through the cracks of the picnic table. When establishing seating arrangements, put the adults on the high side. That way spilled milk doesn't land in their laps.
- Large coolers and ice chests can keep foods cold, but they're cumbersome to carry and a nuisance if you have to buy ice daily. That's why I stick to canned and fresh foods. We use powdered milk for cooking and on cereals, then buy fresh, cold milk just before meals. When everyone drinks it, there's nothing left of a litre at the end of a meal.
- All family members should pitch in and help. Preschool children especially like outdoor dish chores if it means they can play in the sudsy water afterwards.
- Store food safely away from squirrels and night-time visitors. It's a bit of a nuisance to turn the trunk of your car into a larder, but it saves discarding many clawed packages. If you're handy in the workshop, you might make a wooden or metal food box, with a securely fitting lid for carrying food.

Meals while Travelling

Children and restaurants don't always mix. In a strange environment, some children won't eat. To save wasting food, don't order a separate dish for your child, just ask for an extra plate and let him sample from your meal. After, tip generously to compensate the waiter or waitress for the extra work.

Because the meal is produced almost as soon as they come

to the table at home, young children can't understand the wait for service in a restaurant. And although you may let your children leave the table as soon as they've had enough at home, small children are a safety hazard if allowed to crawl, walk or run between tables in a restaurant. A waiter or waitress carrying a tray of dishes can't see below. If he loses his balance, hot coffee from a tray can scald.

No wonder restaurant chains, such as McDonald's, that cater to families with small children are so successful. With a limited menu, food service can be immediate. And on-site playgrounds give parents a couple of minutes peace while they finish their coffee.

Food in these restaurants does have nutritional value. The burger or chicken and bun have plenty of protein, iron and certain essential vitamins. The main problem with fast-food meals is their high fat content — especially if you include the French fries — and salt. The menus also tend to lack vegetables and fruit. This isn't a problem if burger heaven is a once-a-week treat, but if you're on an extended trip, frequent meals in fast-food restaurants can mean your children will be missing out on balanced nutrition.

Strategy for Long Trips

Balance your restaurant meals with snacks of fruit and raw veggies. Make your beverage choice milk or fruit juice instead of soft drinks — even water some of the time. You'll be more successful in counteracting the pop promotions if you set the right example yourself.

More often picnics make sense. Practically every small town has a park with swings and slides. It's either close to the river or the local school. Stop there for your yogurt or cheese, buns or muffins, carrot sticks and apples, juice and milk.

In our family's memory book, one of the best meals I ever made was a breakfast in a park beside the lake in Sault Ste. Marie. The day before, we'd climbed a lookout hill on Manitoulin Island and found a treasure patch of giant wild blueberries. After stuffing ourselves, we still had plenty left over. Even though we stayed at a motel that night, the next morning, instead of heading for a diner we purchased pancake mix, milk and juice at a neighborhood variety store. Using our trusty Coleman stove, we had the best pancakes ever. They were so full of berries that we didn't need syrup.

Neighborhood Treats

Once your offspring can be trusted to visit friends on their own, you're going to be faced with the roving snack gang. At an early age, children try to turn every day into Halloween, especially when they're bored. "We're hungry, Mom. Can we have a cookie?"

In one afternoon that technique can yield oranges at Susan's, chips at Martha's, a fruit drink at John's and cookies from Mrs. O'Reilly. And then you wonder why dinner is such a disaster.

You have some alternatives:

- Give in and schedule dinner for 7 P.M.
- Lay down the law with your youngster. No snacks without checking with you first.
- Negotiate with your neighbors. Together agree on some snack rules — nothing after 5 P.M.; limit snacks to small servings of fruit, cheese and crackers.

I tried this last solution and found I had even more cooperation than I'd expected. The other parents were as worried about the situation as I was.

Dealing with Grandmother

If you were brought up on oatmeal with brown sugar, chances are your mother will try to convince you it's an essential part of a nutritious meal pattern. And if your mother-in-law never gave your spouse candy, she may try to overcompensate with her grandchildren.

When grandmother lives a hundred or more miles away, and visits only at Christmas, birthdays and Easter, you can usually go along with her, and then return to your normal routine when she leaves. But if she's around on a regular basis, you're going to have to choose one of the following strategies:

- be sure you have a good dental plan;
- grin and bear her comments and then play the mean parent when she leaves;
- suggest she read this book and then together discuss your feeding philosophy and ask her to respect your wishes.

If it's sweet treats that are the problem, maybe she just needs some fresh ideas for gifts — coloring or comic books, puzzles, stickers, crayons, markers, balloons or playing cards.

Eating at Nursery School or Daycare

Many nursery schools and daycare centers have excellent programs built around familiar and not-so-familiar foods. Teachers use foods to teach vocabulary, counting, colors, shapes, sizes, measures — a multitude of concepts. They use foods in art to make vegetable prints, edible necklaces, popcorn collages and macaroni pictures.

Unfortunately, however, not all centers realize the importance of nutritious meals, even though food at the daycare center may account for up to fifty percent of a child's energy intake for the day. In 1980, University of Guelph researchers tested the nutrition knowledge of local daycare teachers. The average score was only 10.9 out of a possible 20!

According to a 1985 Federal Provincial Report on Preschoolers, standards for the quality and quantity of food offered in group daycare centers and family daycare operations vary dramatically across Canada. To remedy that problem, nutritionists from the federal and provincial ministries of health published, in 1989, *Canadian Guidelines for Promoting Nutritional Health During the Preschool Years*. It's an excellent resource your daycare center should have.

Meal and snack time at the daycare center can be an ideal feeding situation. Children who shun many foods at home will dig in with their peers. This is a great opportunity to introduce multicultural foods.

As a parent you have a responsibility to take an interest in the meal and snack-time program. What foods are served? How do meals at the daycare center influence your home offerings? Can you gain some new ideas? Can you offer some suggestions and help?

When enrolling your child, ask to see the menus and snack policy. If you're not happy with what is offered, you have some alternatives:

- Take your child elsewhere.
- Offer to help. Suggest that a parents' group plan menus and establish a snacking policy.
- Suggest that the school director seek help. Many health unit nutritionists and dietitians in private practice can offer workshops or menu consulting. The Ontario Milk Marketing Board provides an excellent education program for preschool teachers called "Good Beginnings." Other provincial marketing organizations have resources to share as well.

Snack-time Ideas

In many co-op nursery schools and kindergartens, parents are expected to take turns sending snacks. It will be easiest for everyone if a snacking list is circulated. The best choices are low in sugar to protect baby teeth and first molars. The list can include:

- milk and milk products, such as yogurt (preferably unsweetened) and cheese;
- bread products, such as crackers, bread sticks, tiny muffins;
- pieces of fresh fruit or unsweetened fruit juices;
- pieces of vegetable or vegetable juices;
- portions of hard-cooked egg.

Helping to prepare snacks can be a rotating special project for some of the children. They can spread peanut butter on crackers, stuff celery with processed cheese spread, cut bananas into cubes, cut bread into character shapes with a cookie cutter, and pour juice or milk.

Before They Leave

Daycare teachers often complain that children arrive hungry. Then they haven't the energy to participate in the morning's activities. For breakfast ideas see page 151. Your children will enjoy their breakfast more if you set a good example and join them.

11

THE GRAZING GENERATION

*At the end of the day, a dietitian friend of mine used to
pick up her children at daycare and drive home in
rush hour traffic (which can easily take an hour in
Toronto). She'd then hurry to put dinner on the table
so the children could be eating by six at least.
It wasn't working. "I'd need seat belts on the booster
chairs to keep them still while I rushed about the
kitchen," she complained.
Her solution: Keep nutritious snacks in the car. As
they sit through red light after red light, everyone enjoys
drinking boxes of juice and eating pieces of cheese,
crackers or fruit. Once home, the children are free to
play while Mom soaks in the bathtub to recover her
sanity. Dinner isn't ready until after seven, but no one
minds. By then they are less harried and ready for
social family time and hot food.*

The extended day of many working families makes a three-meals-a-day routine impossible. If your children have a live-in housekeeper, ask her to serve a nutritious "tea-time" snack at five, so that dinner can still be a family affair at seven-thirty or eight. The style of eating whenever and wherever is called grazing.

Is Grazing Dangerous?

Will children become fat? That depends upon the quality of the food they are grazing on. If it's high-fat, high-calorie foods — chips, nuts, snacking cakes, doughnuts, rich cookies — I would be worried. But studies have shown that animals are less likely to overeat when allowed to graze all day than when given the same food in just one or two meals a day. The theory is that your satiety center has time to tell you when you've had enough, before you've overeaten. Also, by nibbling instead of gorging, you don't stretch your stomach.

Will children have a balanced diet? If your children are grazers, it becomes a greater challenge to monitor their diet. On a three-meals-a-day routine, it's relatively easy to plan a balanced diet. All you need do is include foods from at least three of the four food groups in Canada's Food Guide at each meal (pages 90 and 204). But if your children graze, you'll need to evaluate an entire day. I suggest you record all the foods your child eats during a week, then compare to the recommended number of servings.

If all the snacks are typical of the foods listed below, you'll probably find that your child is eating a balanced diet. Dietitian Sandra Matheson makes it easy for her preschoolers. One of the low shelves of her cupboard and part of the refrigerator is devoted to grazers. The children know they can have any of the foods there any time.

Good Grazing Foods

- drinking boxes of fruit and vegetable juices
- individual portion cans of fruit
- unsweetened cereals

- crackers and bread sticks (look for some of the new high-fiber crackers)
- cheese slices or cubes
- plain yogurt
- carrot and celery sticks (already cut)
- nuts (if your child is old enough not to choke — over five years old)
- hard-cooked eggs

Will we lose the social aspects of eating? The family eating experience is very important, but like every aspect of parenting, quality is more important than quantity. For many families, even two meals a day is impossible. In that case, strive for a minimum of one meal with at least one adult present. And make this an unhurried meal, an opportunity for children to share in the happy give-and-take of family dining. Turn off the TV and radio (except for mood music).

The Breakfast Rush

If weekday breakfasts are a rushed affair, make an occasion out of Saturday and Sunday breakfasts. The papers can wait until after the children leave the table.

On weekdays, if you must leave early but your children won't be rushed, pack their breakfast. Let them eat an egg sandwich or muffin and cheese in the car on the way to daycare, or when they arrive at the caregiver's. Some daycare centers even serve breakfast to accommodate these children, although others expect children to arrive well fed.

Fresh Fruit Muffins

1 cup	all-purpose flour	250 mL
1 cup	whole wheat flour	250 mL
½ cup	sugar	125 mL
⅓ cup	instant non-fat dry milk powder	75 mL

1 tbsp	baking powder	15 mL
1/4 tsp	salt	1 mL
1	egg	1
2/3 cup	plain yogurt	150 mL
1/2 cup	low-fat soft margarine, melted and cooled	125 mL
1 cup	fresh fruit, chopped or sliced (strawberries, raspberries, peaches, nectarines, blueberries)	250 mL

In a large bowl, combine all-purpose and whole wheat flours, sugar, milk powder, baking powder and salt. In a medium bowl, beat egg, yogurt and margarine until well blended; stir in fruit. Pour liquid mixture into dry ingredients; stir gently just until dry ingredients are moistened. Spoon batter evenly into 12 lined or greased muffin cups. Bake in a 400°F (200°C) oven 15-20 minutes or until golden brown.

NOTE: Low-fat or calorie-reduced soft margarines contain less fat than normal margarines. To substitute full-fat soft or firm margarines or butter, reduce margarine to 4 tbsp (60 mL) and add 4 tbsp (60 mL) water.

TIP: Add 1/4 tsp (1 mL) cinnamon to dry ingredients when using fruits such as peaches or nectarines.

Yield: 12 muffins.

No-Sugar Muffins
(Blender Method)

Combine and mix in blender:

1	apple, unpeeled but cored	1
1/2 cup	pitted prunes	125 mL
1/2 cup	pitted dates	125 mL
1/4 cup	boiling water	50 mL

Add to above mixture and blend again:

2	small bananas	2
3	eggs	3
¼ cup	butter, softened	50 mL
1 tsp	vanilla	5 mL
1 tsp	salt	5 mL
¼ cup	orange juice	50 mL

In a bowl combine these ingredients:

1½ cup	whole wheat flour	375 mL
1 cup	sunflower seeds	250 mL
1 cup	rolled oats	250 mL
⅓ cup	skim milk powder	75 mL
2 tsp	baking powder	10 mL
1 tsp	baking soda	5 mL
⅓ cup	unsweetened shredded coconut	75 mL

Pour blender mixture over flour mixture. Mix well. Spoon batter into greased muffin cups. Bake at 350°F (180°C) for 20-25 minutes.
Yield: 2-3 dozen muffins.

Pumpkin Oat Bread

2 cups	all-purpose flour	500 mL
1¼ cups	rolled oats (uncooked)	300 mL
1 cup	sugar	250 mL
¼ cup	instant non-fat dry milk powder, optional	50 mL
1 tsp	baking soda	5 mL
½ tsp	baking powder	2 mL
¼ tsp	salt	1 mL
1 tsp	ground cinnamon	5 mL
½ tsp	ground nutmeg	2 mL

¼ tsp	ground cloves	1 mL
2	eggs	2
3 tbsp	vegetable oil	45 mL
1 cup	puréed pumpkin	250 mL
1 cup	plain yogurt	250 mL
½ cup	raisins, finely chopped	125 mL

Grease and line with waxed paper a 9 × 5-in. (2-L) loaf pan.

In a large mixing bowl, combine flour, rolled oats, sugar, milk powder, baking soda, baking powder, salt, cinnamon, nutmeg and cloves. In a separate bowl, beat eggs and oil until light; stir in pumpkin and yogurt. With a spatula, fold in dry ingredients just until well moistened. Fold in raisins. Spoon batter into prepared loaf pan. Bake in a 350°F (180°C) oven 70 minutes or until a tester inserted in center comes out clean. Cool in pan 10 minutes. Remove and cool thoroughly. When cool, wrap tightly and store overnight to mellow flavors.
Yield: 1 loaf.

Dinners for Busy Families

Bulk cooking, freezer meals and microwave cooking are the answers for busy families, especially when not everyone can sit down together. This collection of main dishes includes many family favorites prepared in minimum time.

Quick Microwave Lasagna

½ lb	ground beef	250 g
3½ cups	spaghetti sauce	750 mL
½ cup	water	125 mL
2 cups	cottage cheese (16 oz/500 g)	500 mL
1	egg	1
¼ tsp	pepper	1 mL
8	uncooked lasagna noodles	8
6 oz	sliced mozzarella cheese	175 mL

| ¼ cup | grated Parmesan cheese | 50 mL |

In a large glass bowl, crumble ground beef. Microwave on HIGH (100%) for 2-3 minutes, or until beef is no longer pink; stir once. Drain fat. Stir in spaghetti sauce and water. Meanwhile, combine cottage cheese, egg and pepper. In an 11 × 7-in. (28 × 17-cm) microwave-safe pan, spread ½ cup (125 mL) sauce; alternate layers of noodles (no need to precook), egg mixture, mozzarella cheese and sauce, making 2 layers. Cover with plastic wrap and vent on one side. Microwave on HIGH 8 minutes; then microwave at MEDIUM (50%) 25-30 minutes, or until noodles are fork tender. Carefully remove plastic wrap and sprinkle with Parmesan cheese. Cover and let stand 5-10 minutes.

Conventional cookery: Brown ground beef; drain fat; stir in spaghetti sauce and 1 cup (250 mL) water. In a 12x8-in. (3-L) baking dish, assemble lasagna as directed above. Cover and bake in a 350°F (180°C) oven 50 minutes. Uncover, sprinkle with Parmesan cheese; continue baking 10 minutes or until noodles are tender.
Yield: 6-8 servings.

Chili Soup

1 lb	ground beef	450 g
1	small onion, chopped	1
1	19-oz/540-mL can kidney beans	1
⅓ cup	brown rice	75 mL
2½ cups	tomato juice	625 mL
2½ cups	water	625 mL
1 tbsp	chili powder	15 mL
¼ tsp	salt	1 mL

In a large saucepan, brown ground beef and onion. Drain fat. Stir in kidney beans with can juice, rice, tomato juice, water, chili powder and salt. Bring to a boil; cover, reduce heat and simmer about 45-60 minutes, stirring occasionally. Adjust seasoning to taste with additional chili powder, salt and pepper. Serve hot.

TIP: Children love this soup garnished with grated Cheddar cheese. Crumbled crackers will thicken soup for small children who have a difficult time spooning soup. For a change of pace, serve with tortillas or pita bread instead of crackers.

Freezer Special: Brown 2 lb (900 g) ground beef with doubled quantity of chopped celery and onion. Remove half and mix with soup, vegetables and spices. Spoon into pie plate, cover and freeze for later use. Continue recipe with remaining meat in skillet.

Cover and heat previously frozen meat mixture in a 350°F (180°C) oven 15 minutes or until it bubbles before topping with potatoes as directed below.

Yield: about 9 cups (1.75 L).

Golden Shepherd's Pie

1 lb	lean ground beef, lamb or pork	450 g
2	stalks celery, finely chopped	2
1	small onion, finely chopped	1
1	10-oz/284-mL can tomato or cream of mushroom or cream of celery soup	1
2½ cups	frozen mixed vegetables or leftover cooked vegetables (carrots, corn, peas, green beans, turnips)	625 mL
¼-½ tsp	herbs or spice, optional	1-2 mL
4	medium potatoes, peeled and quartered	4

¼ cup	instant non-fat dry milk powder	50 mL
¼ cup	grated Parmesan cheese	50 mL
1 cup	shredded Cheddar cheese	250 mL

In a skillet, brown ground meat with celery and onion. Drain fat. Stir in soup, vegetables and herbs, if desired; heat mixture until it bubbles; adjust seasoning to taste; reduce heat and keep warm until ready to assemble pie.

Cook potatoes in lightly salted water until tender; drain, reserving ¼ cup (50 mL) of cooking liquid. Mash potatoes; blend in reserved cooking liquid, milk powder and Parmesan cheese.

Spoon meat mixture into a lightly greased 9-in. (1-L) pie plate. Spread potatoes over meat, covering to edges of pie plate. Bake in a 350°F (180°C) oven 15 minutes. Remove and top with Cheddar cheese; return to oven for 5-8 minutes until golden.

NOTE: Herbs or spice are based on meat used. They reduce the need for salt. For beef, use dried parsley or chili powder; for lamb, dried oregano or rosemary; for pork, dried thyme.

TIP: If your family doesn't all eat at the same time, you may want to make small individual pies, instead of one family-sized pie.

Yield: 4-6 servings.

Pizza Pork

This is a good way to enjoy the pizza flavor without the pepperoni and crust, which children often don't eat. When pork shoulder or leg roast is "on special," buy a large roast. Cut off about 2 cups (500 mL) for this recipe, and then serve the roast at another meal.

1 lb	boneless lean pork shoulder or leg	450 g

1-2 tbsp	vegetable oil	15-30 mL
1	clove garlic, finely chopped	1
1	medium onion, chopped	1
1	medium green pepper, chopped	1
4 oz	small, fresh mushrooms, sliced	100 g
½ tsp	each of dried thyme and oregano leaves	2 mL
1 cup	tomato sauce or spaghetti sauce	250 mL
½ cup	water	125 mL
	Hot cooked noodles, spaghetti or rice	
1 cup	grated mozzarella cheese, divided	250 mL

Cut pork into ½-in. (1.5-cm) cubes, trimming off any fat or gristle. In a large skillet, heat oil; add pork and garlic, stir-fry over medium heat just until pork is no longer pink. Add onion, green pepper, mushrooms, thyme and oregano. Stir-fry 3 minutes longer. Add tomato sauce and water; bring to a boil, reduce heat and simmer, partially covered, 20-25 minutes.

Place noodles on serving plates and sprinkle with half of mozzarella cheese, spoon on meat sauce and top with remaining cheese. If desired, heat in warm oven or microwave until cheese melts. Serve immediately.

TIP: Trim and cut pork cubes when pork is purchased. (Smaller cubes if you have very young children, larger cubes for older children.) Store in refrigerator or freezer for a quick-to-prepare meal.

NOTE: A can of mushrooms, drained, may be substituted for

fresh mushrooms, but should not be added until last 10 minutes of cooking. Toast can be substituted for the pasta or rice.
Yield: 4-6 servings.

Two-Meal Chicken

When your supermarket features chickens, buy a large frying chicken (3-4 lb/1.4 to 1.8 kg). Pull the skin back to cut off the majority of breast, thigh and leg meat keeping the pieces as large as possible. Use boneless chicken for Parmesan Chicken or Chicken Nuggets, and the remaining chicken and giblets for Gonzo's Chicken Soup, which contains garbanzo beans (chick peas) as a supplementary source of protein.

Gonzo's Chicken Soup

½	chicken, about 1½ lb/680 g, or chicken remaining from Two Meal Chicken	½
6 cups	water	1.5 L
	Tops (leaves) from 3 stalks celery	
½ tsp	thyme	2 mL
2 cups	chopped celery	500 mL
1½ cups	finely chopped carrot	375 mL
1	small onion, chopped	1
1	19-oz/540-mL can garbanzo beans (chick peas)	1
⅓ cup	small soup pasta or broken spaghetti	75 mL
¼ cup	chopped fresh parsley	50 mL
2 tbsp	lime or lemon juice	25 mL
1 tsp	celery salt	5 mL

Cut chicken into pieces. In a large saucepan or Dutch oven, combine chicken (including giblets but excluding liver), water, celery tops and thyme. Heat to boiling; reduce heat; simmer, covered, about 45 minutes, or until chicken is tender. Remove chicken and discard celery tops. Add ½ cup (125 mL) ice cubes to broth to force fat to rise to surface; skim off fat. Separate meat from bones and skin; cut meat into small pieces; refrigerate.

Add celery, carrot and onion to broth in saucepan; bring to a boil; simmer 5 minutes. Add garbanzo beans and pasta; continue cooking 15 minutes, or until pasta is tender. Return chicken to saucepan along with parsley, lime juice and celery salt. Heat to serving temperature. Adjust seasoning to taste.

Yield: about 10 cups (2.5 L).

Chicken Parmesan

2	boneless chicken breasts	2
	All-purpose flour	
1	egg, beaten	1
1 tbsp	soft butter or margarine	15 mL
½ cup	Oven Coating (page 113)	125 mL
2 slices	mozzarella cheese	2 slices
⅓ cup	spaghetti or tomato sauce, heated	75 mL

Place chicken between sheets of waxed paper; with a mallet, pound chicken to a uniform thickness, about ¼ in. (3 mm). Coat chicken with flour. Dip in beaten egg. Dip in Oven Coating until well covered. Place coated chicken on a greased baking sheet. Bake in a 400°F (200°C) oven 12 minutes. Brush with butter, turn and brush second side. Return to oven 12-15 minutes or until golden and tender. Top each piece with cheese and return to oven just until cheese melts. Serve immediately, topped with spaghetti sauce.

TIP: For young children, cut each breast piece in half or in strips and reduce cooking time.

Yield: 2-3 servings.

Oven Chicken Nuggets

½ lb	boneless chicken (thigh, leg or breast)	225 g
	All-purpose flour	
1	egg, beaten	1
2 tbsp	evaporated milk or light cream	25 mL
1 cup	Oven Coating (page 113)	250 mL
1 tbsp	vegetable oil	25 mL
	Spaghetti or barbecue sauce	

Cut chicken into pieces of uniform size and thickness. Coat with flour. Dip floured chicken in a mixture of egg and milk; drain. Coat pieces with Oven Coating. Coat bottom of a large baking dish with vegetable oil. Place coated chicken in dish allowing ample room between pieces. Bake in a 400°F (200°C) oven, turning 2 or 3 times, 20-30 minutes or until chicken is tender. (Baking time is determined by size of chicken pieces.) Serve warm with spaghetti or barbecue sauce for dipping.

TIP: If youngsters like lots of crispy coating, double dip the pieces in the egg and crumb mixtures.

Yield: 2-4 servings.

12
VEGETARIAN EATING

Vegetarian eating — some or all the time — is growing in popularity. Less expensive vegetarian meals help families control their food budget. And for families concerned about the health risks associated with higher fat diets, going vegetarian allows them to concentrate more on high-carbohydrate legumes and grains. In addition, in some families vegetarian eating is part of a religious or philosophical lifestyle.

When carefully planned, vegetarian meals can be very nutritious and healthy. But when taken to an extreme, vegetarianism can also leave children severely malnourished and prone to diseases such as nutritional rickets and anemia. Some young children have even died because their parents didn't realize that when they eliminated entire groups of foods from the menu, they also removed important sources of some vitamins and minerals.

To feed children, especially babies and toddlers, well on a vegetarian pattern you'll need a greater understanding of the nutrition issues than the average parent, and you'll have to carefully balance menus.

Different Kinds of Vegetarianism

The degree of risk depends upon the form of vegetarianism practiced. The chart that follows compares some of the traditional forms of vegetarianism.

Pure vegan, fruitarian and macrobiotic diets are not appropriate for young children. These diets do not allow animal products, with the exception of breast-milk. Children's small stomachs don't have the capacity to handle enough of the bulky, fibrous plant foods needed to meet all their energy, protein and fat needs. On such diets children are clearly malnourished. Growth is retarded; children develop iron and vitamin B12 anemia, and vitamin D deficiency rickets. They frequently become ill, and many have died from recurrent infections such as pneumonia.

Forms of Vegetarianism

Foods Eaten	Potential Deficiencies	Comments
Lacto-ovo-vegetarian		
Vegetables, fruits, nuts, grains, legumes, milk, milk products, eggs	iron, zinc	Can be adequate at all stages of life. Risk for children is minimal.
Lacto-vegetarian		
As above, but without eggs	iron, zinc, vitamin B12	Can be adequate, but need to be sure to use iron-enriched infant cereals.

Foods Eaten	Potential Deficiencies	Comments
Vegan Vegetables, fruits, nuts, grains, legumes	iron, zinc, calories, riboflavin, calcium, vitamin D, vitamin B12	Not recommended for infants and young children.
Fruitarian Raw or dried fruit, nuts, honey, oil	protein, calories, vitamins A, D, B12, and folic acid; minerals calcium, phosphorus, iodine, and iron	Not recommended for infants, children or adults.
Macrobiotic Adherents to it progress through 10 stages: lower stages allow cereals, fruits, vegetables and some animal products; purer and higher stages allow only brown rice. Liquids are avoided at all stages.	The higher the stage, the more inadequate this diet becomes. Can be deficient in any of the nutrients listed under Vegan or Fruitarian	Children's deaths have been attributed to this diet.

As a nutritionist, I strongly support families deciding to follow a semi-vegetarian or a lacto-ovo-vegetarian pattern. For the rest of this chapter, the term vegetarian will refer to those patterns only.

Nutritional Ramifications of Vegetarian Eating

Energy and Fat

If you've ever studied calorie charts, you'll have noticed that the calorie-dense foods are the foods that contain fat — ice cream, full-fat cheese, meat and, of course, rich baked goods and fried foods. On the other hand, vegetables, fruits, breads and cereals tend to contain more water and fewer calories. For that reason, vegetarian meal patterns are generally low calorie and low in fat. That's certainly a benefit for most adults. But babies and young children need calories for growth, as well as a certain amount of fat for cell and nerve growth. Human milk is high in fat, protein and many of the nutrients needed for healthy growth, provided the mother is adequately nourished herself. Once weaned off breast-milk or infant formula, vegetarian babies should continue to be given homogenized milk.

Protein

The advantage of animal-based protein foods such as meat, fish, eggs, milk and dairy products is that the protein in these foods is complete. That means these proteins have all the component amino acids in the proportions needed by humans. But protein foods of vegetable origin — nuts, legumes and cereals — lack one or more of these essential amino acids. Still, vegetarians make good use of these vegetable protein sources by mixing and matching so that they end up with a complete protein pair at the same meal. For example, if a legume that lacks one essential amino acid is eaten at the same meal as a cereal that lacks a different amino acid, the two combine to make a complete protein mixture. Baked beans and bread, or dhal and rice, are examples of these combinations.

Alternatively, a small amount of animal protein (for example, cheese) can be added to legumes to provide the missing amino acids. That's why this Rice and Bean Pie makes such a nutritious supper. If you start with canned kidney beans and cook in the microwave, this recipe proves that vegetarian cooking need not be more time-consuming.

Rice and Bean Pie

¾ cup	long grain rice	175 mL
2 tbsp	butter or margarine	25 mL
1½ cups	sliced onions	375 mL
½ cup	diced celery	125 mL
½ cup	cooked kidney beans	125 mL
½ cup	milk	125 mL
2	eggs, slightly beaten	2
1 cup	grated Colby or Cheddar cheese	250 mL
½ tsp	salt	2 mL
½ tsp	tarragon	2 mL
Dash	Worcestershire sauce	Dash

Cook rice and drain. Melt butter; cook onions and celery until soft but not brown. In a large bowl, combine onions and celery, cooked rice, beans, milk, eggs, cheese and seasonings. Spoon into a greased quiche pan or a 10-in. (1.5-L) pie plate. Bake in a 325°F (160°C) oven 25-30 minutes or until set.

Microwave: Assemble as above, microwave on HIGH (100%) 5 minutes, then at MEDIUM-HIGH (70%) 5 minutes. Let stand 5 minutes before serving.
Yield: 4-6 servings.

Fiber

Sometimes mixtures of finely powdered nuts and puréed legumes used as vegetarian protein sources have too much fiber and are too bulky for small babies. They will suffer from gas, bloated stomachs and rashes from too many dirty diapers.

That's why, for young children, these vegetable protein foods must be balanced with eggs, tofu, tahini and cheese. (Remember to use just egg yolk, without the white, for infants under a year of age.)

Iron

Meat is an important source of iron, but there are other iron sources for your vegetarian baby — egg yolk, iron-fortified infant cereals, green vegetables and legumes.

Vitamin B12

This vitamin is found only in animal-based foods such as milk and egg yolk. If only small amounts of these foods are used, a supplement is necessary. The alternative is to use a soy-based milk substitute that contains added vitamin B12.

Vitamin D

Infants, particularly during the winter months, don't have much opportunity for exposure to direct sunlight. For this reason, the added vitamin D in milk and infant formulas is necessary. Vegetarian babies not given milk lack this nutrient and may develop vitamin D deficiency rickets.

Further Reading

I can't really do justice to the nutrition facts you should know if planning to feed your children regularly on a vegetarian pattern. Therefore, I recommend you also read a good book on the subject. Look for:

- *New Laurel's Kitchen: A Handbook on Vegetarian Cookery and Nutrition* by L. Robertson and others (Ten Speed Press, 1986).
- *On the Road to Vegetarian Cooking*, written by Canadian Anne Lukin (Second Story Press, 1991).
- *Moosewood Cookbook* (revised edition) by Mollie Katzen

(Ten Speed Press, 1992).

- *The Inspired Vegetarian* by Louise Pickford (Stewart, Tabori & Chang, 1992).

Vegetarian Recipes

I asked Carolyn Clark, a British Columbia dietitian and mother of two preschool children, to share her vegetarian recipes. Carolyn has followed a lacto-ovo-vegetarian pattern since her teenage years so she knows what she's talking about.

Carolyn says vegetarian cooking is "a matter of common sense." You can often improvise successfully by substituting legumes and nuts for the meat in many of your standard recipes. For example, add chopped tofu to salads, just as you would hard-cooked eggs. In pizza, use cashews instead of shrimp or sausage. Sliced eggplant and a cheese slice, breaded and fried as you would a veal cutlet, makes a vegetarian schnitzel.

Even if your family doesn't follow a vegetarian pattern, you will find Carolyn's recipes economical, delicious and a welcome change.

Pecan Patties

Large pecan patties are terrific as burgers. Use smaller ones as meatballs in your spaghetti sauce. Carolyn prepares them in large batches for freezing. They reheat in the microwave in about 2 minutes, or you can bake them in a tomato sauce at 350°F (180°C) for about 25 minutes.

1 cup	fine dry bread crumbs	250 mL
1 cup	ground pecans	250 mL
1 cup	grated Cheddar cheese	250 mL
1	large onion, chopped	1
5	large eggs, beaten	5
½ tsp	dried sage	2 mL
½ tsp	dried basil	2 mL

¼ tsp	salt	1 mL
Pinch	pepper	Pinch
	Corn oil	

Combine all ingredients and shape into patties. Fry in hot oil until brown on both sides.

Yield: about 12 medium-sized patties.

Mexican Loaf

1	14-oz/398-mL can kidney beans, drained	1
2 cups	Cheddar cheese, grated	500 mL
1	onion, chopped fine	1
1 tbsp	melted butter	15 mL
1 cup	fine dry bread crumbs	250 mL
2	large eggs, beaten	2
⅛ tsp	basil	½ mL
⅛ tsp	oregano	½ mL
⅛ tsp	poultry seasoning	½ mL
1	green pepper, cut in rings	1
1	7½-oz/213-mL can tomato sauce	1

In a food processor, process beans briefly. Add the cheese to the beans and blend briefly. Sauté onion in butter until soft. Add the beans, bread crumbs, eggs and seasonings to the onions and mix well. Line the bottom of an 8½ × 4½-in. (21 × 11-cm) loaf pan with foil. Butter the foil and sides of the pan. Pack the bean mixture firmly into the loaf pan. Bake at 350°F (180°C) 35 minutes, or until brown. Garnish with green pepper rings and serve hot with heated tomato sauce.

Veggie Pizza

The pizza dough recipe below makes enough for two pizzas. If you like, you can freeze half the dough for later use. When

you don't have time to make the crust from scratch, use refrigerated biscuit mix instead. You can add a little wheat germ
to the mix for extra nutrition.

Crust:

1	package active dry yeast	1
1 cup	warm water	250 mL
1¼ cups	whole wheat flour	300 mL
1½ cups	all-purpose flour	375 mL
½ tsp	salt	2 mL
1 tbsp	salad oil	15 mL

Dissolve yeast in water. In a medium bowl, combine flours
and salt. Make a well in the center and pour in yeast and oil.
Mix until well blended. Turn out dough onto floured surface.
Knead until very smooth and elastic, kneading in additional
flour if dough is too sticky. Place dough in a greased bowl.
Grease surface of dough and cover with a towel. Let rise in
warm place until doubled in bulk, about one hour.

Punch down dough and divide in half. Freeze one half for
another time. Roll remaining dough to fit a 12-in. (30.5-cm)
pizza pan.

Sauce:

1	7½-oz/213-mL can tomato sauce	1
Pinch	dried oregano	Pinch
	Garlic salt	
	Freshly ground pepper	

Combine tomato sauce and spices. Spread over crust.

Toppings:

½ cup	chopped onion	125 mL
½ cup	chopped celery	125 mL
2 tsp	vegetable oil	10 mL
½ cup	sliced mushrooms	125 mL

½ cup	chopped unsalted roasted cashews	125 mL
	Black olives	
2 cups	mozzarella cheese, grated	500 mL
	Parmesan cheese, grated	

Sauté onion and celery in oil until onion is transparent. Sprinkle onion over tomato sauce. Arrange mushrooms, cashews and black olives on top of sauce. Sprinkle with mozzarella and Parmesan cheese. Bake at 400°F (200°C) for about 15 minutes.

Ratatouille Lasagna

This mixture of Italian and Middle Eastern flavors is a wonderful way to disguise "weird" vegetables children wouldn't normally eat. Carolyn prefers spinach lasagna noodles, or the new oven-ready ones. But even before these came on the market, she never bothered to precook the noodles; she just used a little extra sauce.

1	clove garlic	1
1	medium onion, diced	1
1 tsp	cumin	5 mL
1 tsp	vegetable oil	5 mL
1	small eggplant, cubed	1
1	medium zucchini, quartered lengthwise and sliced	1
6	fresh mushrooms, sliced	6
1	14-oz/398-mL can stewed tomatoes	1
2 cups	ricotta cheese	500 mL
3½ oz	Parmesan cheese	100 g
2	eggs	2
1 tsp	nutmeg	5 mL
2 tsp	basil	10 mL

| 11 oz | tomato sauce, divided | 350 mL |
| 10 oz | mozzarella cheese, grated | 300 g |

Ratatouille Mixture: Sauté garlic, onion and cumin in oil. When onions are soft and transparent, add eggplant, zucchini and mushrooms. Continue cooking until oil is absorbed and vegetables are soft, about 15 minutes. Add tomatoes. Simmer until moisture is absorbed and eggplant has become slightly mushy, about 20 minutes.

Ricotta Layer: Combine ricotta and Parmesan cheeses, eggs and nutmeg and basil.

Assembly: In a 12 × 8-in. (3-L) baking dish, layer 5 oz (150 mL) of the tomato sauce, the ricotta layer, lasagna noodles, the ratatouille mixture, another layer of lasagna noodles, 6 oz (200 mL) tomato sauce and finally 10 oz (300 g) mozzarella cheese, grated. Bake at 350°F (180°C) 1 hour. Let stand 10 minutes before cutting.

Yield: 6-8 servings

13

FOOD ALLERGIES AND
FOOD INTOLERANCES

Living with food allergies or food intolerances isn't easy. But it's even harder living with children with food allergies — their reactions are often much more severe. Besides, it's hard to watch your child suffer, or to prevent her from eating certain foods.

Any parent who has walked the floor night after night with a colicky baby, tried to comfort a wheezing infant, fought a losing battle with her baby's diaper rash, or told a preschooler she can't have a piece of birthday cake knows what I mean. Thankfully, most infant reactions to foods are food sensitivities, not allergies; they usually last only a few months.

But some children do develop true food allergies that can last throughout life. In true food allergy, certain food components, usually proteins, act as allergens. When ingested, these allergens trigger chemical reactions in the body. The body acts as if the food is a poison; it produces antibodies to fight off the allergen and in the process potent chemicals, such as histamines, are released. It's these histamines that cause the digestive problems, skin rashes, swelling of the lips and mouth, shortness of breath, even shock.

With repeated exposure to the allergen, the reactions may

become more severe. Ideally, we'd like to prevent infants from ever having an allergic reaction. In the first four to six months of life, a baby's intestinal tract is somewhat "leaky," allowing large protein molecules to be absorbed. Exclusive breast-feeding and delayed introduction of solid foods reduces your baby's exposure to many large proteins which could be potential allergens.

If formula, some or all of the time, is necessary, your doctor may recommend a product such as Carnation "Good Start," in which the protein molecules have been predigested to reduce the allergy potential. Soy formulas are not recommended as they can cause allergies.

As your baby's diet changes, introduce all foods gradually. Symptoms such as a rash, diarrhea or stomach cramps after introducing a new food may be unrelated, but it's best to be on the safe side. Avoid that food for about a month, then try it again when your baby is older and healthier.

Wheat cereals, regular cow's milk, egg white and orange juice are the most common allergens in the first year of life. The most dangerous allergies are to peanuts and peanut butter, nuts and shellfish. If your child ever experiences breathing difficulties or swelling of the lips or face, seek medical help immediately.

Accurate diagnosis of allergies in children is difficult, but important. Many children suffer needlessly from recurrent diarrhea, stomach cramps, hives and eczema when a change in diet could help.

When twenty-two-month-old Laurie was brought to Nan Millette, a dietitian at Toronto's Hospital for Sick Children, she was underweight. Her parents complained that she wasn't eating well and said that Laurie was allergic to milk, peanut butter, jam, ketchup, fish and chocolate. Nan, however, found that Laurie was having milk on her cereal and cheese and yogurt frequently. Also she was having about thirty ounces of apple juice every day. If Laurie had a true allergy to milk, she wouldn't be able to tolerate the milk on her cereal or cheese. Nan helped the parents plan a more balanced menu which includes less juice and more milk, including homogenized milk on her cereal. A few months later, Laurie was eating well and gaining weight.

In all likelihood, when Laurie's parents brought her to the dietitian, her appetite was down because she was at a plateau stage in her growth. But at this stage, Laurie's parents needed help determining which foods, if any, Laurie was really allergic to. A restricted diet may be the correct cautious approach for a short period of time. But check back with your doctor later. You may be able to reintroduce some of the restricted foods.

I am particularly concerned about the nutritional well-being of some children who have been put on very restrictive diets by unqualified, self-professed allergy specialists.

Be suspect of test results and advice, if the allergist

- isn't a bona fide member of the Canadian Society of Allergy;
- uses bizarre tests (rather than taking a diet history) to diagnose allergens;
- blames failing school grades and poor behavior on allergies.

In case of any of the above, it's time for another opinion. Talk to your family physician.

Nonallergic Food Sensitivities

Sometimes dietary restrictions are necessary for other sensitivities that are not true allergies.

Lactose Intolerance

Lactose intolerance results from an inherited lack of the enzyme lactase. This enzyme is necessary to break down milk sugar (lactose) before it can be digested. Symptoms of vomiting, diarrhea, bloating and stomach cramps occur after drinking milk or eating milk-containing foods. Lactose intolerance is more likely to occur in older children or adults. Lacteeze, a two-percent milk from which lactose has been removed, is available in many areas of Canada. Lacteeze has all the protein, calcium and vitamins normally in milk. The sugar, however, has been predigested, or turned into a form that is well tolerated by lactose-intolerant individuals. You can even bake with Lacteeze.

Celiac Disease

Celiac disease is an inability to metabolize gluten, a protein found in wheat, oats, barley and rye. Symptoms include serious diarrhea, bloating and cramps. Children with this disease must avoid all foods, including common breads and cereals, made from wheat flour, oats, barley or rye. Fortunately special gluten-free breads are available at certain specialized bakeries and food stores.

Phenylketonuria

Other rarer problems result from an inability to metabolize certain components of protein. For example, children with phenylketonuria cannot handle the amino acid phenylalanine. Very special diets are needed for these children.

Attitude Is Important

When food allergies are first diagnosed parents can approach the news with relief ("Now, I can do something to make my child's life easier") or they can react with pity ("How will I cope with a special diet?"). The family who cheerfully meets the problem head on, with creativity, is on its way to producing healthy, well-adjusted children. One such creative mother shared her solution for Halloween. When her allergic child brings home the loot bag, he's allowed to barter the forbidden candies for crayons, erasers and small toys.

Help Is Available

If a qualified expert finds that your child does have a food allergy, you'll need some help. Ask a professional dietitian to show you how to plan your child's diet around the permitted foods, look for certain ingredients on food labels and suggest food substitutes. She can assess this meal pattern to see if supplements are necessary to make up for the foods that will be missing.

For recipes, moral support from other parents and ongoing information on food products, I enthusiastically recommend joining the Allergy and Asthma Information Association, 65 Tromley Drive, Ste. 10, Etobicoke, Ont. M9B 5Y7. They have regular newsletters, conferences and useful resource materials. In this chapter is a sampling of recipes from their two cookbooks, *Diets Unlimited for Limited Diets* and *Foods for Festive Occasions*.

You can buy wheat-free, gluten-free, milk-free, egg-free and other special foods from the Specialty Food Shop, 23 College St., Toronto, Ont. M5G 2B3. They offer national mail-order service from 875 Main St. W., Hamilton, Ont. L8S 4R1. Many children's hospitals also sell diet products in their gift shops.

Banana Pancakes
(Free of milk, wheat, corn and gluten.)

| 1 | banana | 1 |
| 1 | egg | 1 |

Mash banana, add egg and mix. Fry in a hot, oiled pan 5 minutes on each side. Turn carefully. Serve with or without syrup.
Yield: 1 serving.

Potato Flour Waffles
(Free of wheat, corn and gluten.)

1 cup	potato flour	250 mL
2 tsp	baking powder	10 mL
¾ tsp	salt	3 mL
2	eggs, separated	2
3 tbsp	vegetable oil	40 mL
¾ cup	milk	175 mL

Sift dry ingredients together. In a separate bowl, beat egg whites until stiff. In another bowl, beat egg yolks, then blend in oil and milk. Stir in dry ingredients, beating until mixture thickens. Fold in stiffly beaten egg whites. Drop by spoonfuls onto waffle iron and bake.
Yield: 3-5 square waffles.

Chocolate Mousse
(Free of eggs, wheat, corn, gluten.)

1 tbsp	unflavored gelatin	15 mL
2 cups	cold milk, divided	500 mL
1	square unsweetened chocolate	1
¼ tsp	salt	1 mL
½ tsp	vanilla extract	2 mL
6 tsp	sugar	30 mL
	Whipped cream	

Soften gelatin in ½ cup (125 mL) cold milk. Heat remainder of milk. When hot, add chocolate and continue heating, without letting milk boil, until chocolate has melted.

Add gelatin mixture to chocolate milk, and heat just below

boiling point. Remove from heat and mix in salt, vanilla and sugar. Chill about 1½ hours or until firm.

Beat mixture until it is fluffy, divide among serving dishes and return to refrigerator. Decorate with whipped cream.
Yield: four ½-cup (125-mL) servings.

Barley Pilaf
(Free of eggs, wheat, corn.)

2 tbsp	butter or margarine	25 mL
2 tbsp	chopped onion	25 mL
1 cup	pearl barley	250 mL
	Salt and pepper, to taste	
2 cups	beef bouillon	500 mL
2 cups	water	500 mL

Heat butter in a skillet and add onion. Cook over low heat for 5 minutes. Add barley and cook, stirring until grains are covered with butter and lightly browned. Add seasoning. Place in a well-greased 2-qt (2-L) casserole. Mix beef bouillon and water to total 4 cups (1 L) of liquid. Pour over casserole to cover barley by ½ in. (1 cm). Cover casserole and bake at 325°F (160°C) 35 minutes. Remove cover and add remaining liquid and continue cooking, uncovered, 30 minutes or until barley is tender and liquid is absorbed.
Yield: six to seven ½-cup (125-mL) servings.

Sponge Cake
(Free of wheat, gluten and corn.)

6	eggs (at room temperature)	6
1 cup	sugar	250 mL
½ cup	instant non-fat dry milk	125 mL
1 tbsp	lemon juice	15 mL
½ tsp	salt	2 mL

1 cup	rice flour	250 mL
Topping:		
1	10-oz/284-g package frozen raspberries (thawed)	1
½ cup	orange juice	125 mL
1 cup	whipping (35%) cream	250 mL
1-2 tsp	sugar, optional	5-10 mL

Blend eggs, 1 cup (250 mL) sugar, milk powder, lemon juice and salt in a large bowl. Beat at high speed, until mixture holds in soft peaks, 15-20 minutes. Beat rice flour, a tablespoon at a time, into mixture. Scrape sides of bowl often. Rinse a 10-in. (25-cm) tube pan with cold water. Pour batter into pan and bake 50-60 minutes at 350°F (180°C). Cake surface should spring back when gently pressed. Turn pan upside down. Remove cake when cool and place on plate.

About an hour before serving, thoroughly drain juice from berries. Mix this juice with orange juice. Spoon juices over cake and let soak in; be careful not to saturate cake too much. Whip cream, adding sugar if desired. Frost top and sides of cake. Drain berries on paper towelling. Decorate top of cake with the berries.

Yield: 1 cake.

14

SPECIAL FEEDING NEEDS
OF DISABLED CHILDREN

Disabled children have all the usual requirements for good care and feeding. In addition, they have some special needs, some of which are the same as those of other children recovering from an illness or getting ready for an operation. Thus, although I've written this chapter primarily to provide some practical ideas for parents and caregivers of disabled children, I think some of the ideas will be useful at times for all parents.

Eating requires considerable physical dexterity and coordination. A child must learn to pick up food with her fingers or a utensil, guide the food into her mouth, close her lips to ensure no food or liquid falls back out, use her tongue to manipulate the food from side to side, open and close the jaw with a rotary motion for chewing, bring the food or liquid back together in a bolus and roll it to the back of the mouth with her tongue in preparation for swallowing. Swallowing involves closing off the pharynx to prevent food from entering the airway just prior to the food entering the esophagus and finally opening the airway again.

It all sounds very complicated. Some of the steps are directed by voluntary muscle control, some by involuntary reflexes. For the child with a physical or mental disability, learning to co-ordinate the muscles necessary to chew and swallow can be a slow and difficult task. And for some children with swallowing disorders, the involuntary actions may not occur.

A child's eating disorders range from difficulty in learning to manipulate food to his mouth, or drooling because it's difficult to close his lips, to the risk of aspirating food or liquid. Aspiration occurs when food or liquid travels down the airway, past the vocal cords. If the food or liquid doesn't cause choking, it can cause pneumonia.

Because there is such a range of possible problems, the first step prior to treatment should be thorough assessment by trained professionals — physicians, physical therapists and di-etitians specializing in eating and swallowing disorders. Any baby or child who fails to gain weight; coughs, gags or wheezes when given solids; experiences heartburn at every meal; or has been fed by a nasogastric tube for more than five weeks should be assessed for feeding problems. And to be most effective, this should be done early — by the time the baby is six to nine months old. A thorough assessment requires a battery of tests by a team of specialists. It is usually done in major treatment centers such as the Hospital for Sick Children in Toronto.

Too often, appropriate help is not given. Children miss cru-cial learning opportunities that would help them advance from dependent to independent feeding. Others are malnourished and dehydrated because the feeding and swallowing process takes so long that not enough food is given.

This, or any other book, cannot replace individual assess-ment and training. What I have included in this chapter are some practical ideas caregivers may want to try with the dis-abled children in their care.

Learning to Eat Is Important

A child who is an uncoordinated or messy eater is often isolated from others. He misses out on important social interaction and can easily become spoiled.

As well, learning to manipulate lips, tongue and jaw are important first steps in your baby's learning to speak.

The objective of a long-term feeding training program should be to help the child progress as far as possible towards self-feeding. But that must be done without compromising his nutritional status. If many hours a day are spent eating, but the child remains undernourished and uncomfortable, then other options for adequate nutrition should be used.

Learning to Suck

For most babies sucking is a natural reflex that starts before birth. X-rays have shown babies sucking their thumb in the womb. Most babies can begin sucking their mother's breast or a nipple the day they're born.

However, a baby with a cleft lip or palate will have difficulty maintaining a vacuum in his mouth for suction. Breast-feeding is often the best alternative because the delivery of milk doesn't require suction. But it may be slow. The vacuum can sometimes be improved by placing a finger over the cleft in the lip or by nursing the baby with the affected side next to the breast.

If breast-feeding is too slow, you may want to supplement with a bottle, spoon or dropper, using your own expressed milk. But where possible, maintain some nursing at every feeding, as it encourages the development of normal facial muscles.

If nursing isn't possible, there are special cleft lip and palate nursers, or you can use a soft nipple with large holes. (Boil new nipples to soften them.) Be sure to ask for appropriate advice and help on feeding your baby before leaving the hospital.

For older children with disabilities, learning to suck from a straw makes drinking liquids neater. Also, drinking from a straw helps develop better lip closure and lip pressure.

To teach this skill, dip a plastic straw into some liquid your child likes. Place a finger over the top of the straw to keep the liquid in, and place the bottom of the straw in the child's mouth. You may have to help him close his lips around the straw. By releasing your finger on the straw, a little at a time, you can control the flow of liquid into his mouth, until he learns to suck.

Desensitizing His Mouth

Hypersensitivity around the mouth is often seen in cerebral palsy children. But this may just be the result of having missed an important learning period — that stage when baby puts everything in his mouth, including toys and fingers.

If your baby can't reach his own mouth, you will have to help him become accustomed to objects touching his face, lips and mouth. Do it slowly, but with firm pressure rather than a light tickle. In play and in washing, gradually accustom him to your touch, starting away from his face and gradually working closer to his mouth. A soft cloth or terry cloth towel in washing and drying provides good stimulation.

If your child is hypersensitive, you may have to be sneaky to get inside his mouth. Pretend to search for a bite of cookie that he's just eaten. After he's let you feel around with your index finger to see if it's all gone, reward him with another bite. Regularly ask to count his teeth to see if there are any new ones.

Learning Tongue Control

Tongue-control exercises can be fun. Put some sweet or sticky foods on one or other side of the palate and have Tommy Tongue find it and make it disappear. Use graham crackers or other foods of similar consistency that can be felt in different parts of the mouth, if your child can handle them without choking.

Ice cream, or other treats on his lips, helps teach him to move his tongue between his teeth.

Opening and Closing Her Mouth

If you need to support her head and help her close her mouth when eating, sit on her right side. Then you can put your arm around behind her head and support her jaw with your left hand.

Your middle finger should be placed under the child's chin, just behind the boney portion of the chin. The finger should lie flat and should not choke or gouge her. Its purpose is to help keep the jaw closed and stop the tongue from pushing the food out.

Place your index finger on the chin itself, just below the lower lip. That way you can open the jaw slightly to introduce food, and assist the child in using her lower lip. For stability rest your thumb on the side of her head, just below her eye.

Work slowly, and don't force the child's mouth open.

If your child has good head control, you can control her jaw from the front, using your non-feeding hand to help her open and close her mouth. In this position use your middle finger to assist jaw closure, and your thumb on her chin to assist opening. Your index finger on her cheek provides support.

Learning to Chew

You may have to manipulate the child's jaw, with your hands on his cheeks to show him the up and down movements of chewing. Use foods that will be broken down by the saliva anyway, so he won't gag if the chewing isn't successful — small chunks of cooked vegetables or fruits, such as potatoes or apple, or teething biscuits.

When feeding a cleft palate child, avoid foods that might become lodged in the palate opening — peanut butter, peelings of raw fruits, leafy vegetables, creamed dishes and, of course, nuts.

Teaching Swallowing

Start with smooth purées and a small spoon. Keep portions very small as more than ⅓ teaspoon can cause gagging and choking if it enters the airway. Touch the spoon to the child's lips and wait for her to open her mouth. Place some food on the back of her tongue, remove the spoon and help her close her lips. Then gently stroke her throat downward from just below her chin to her chest.

Between bites, allow for dry or cleansing swallows (no food). If she coughs or gags, allow her to do this, without panicking. Coughing is a necessary reflex to prevent food from entering the airway. If caregivers react to each cough, it can become an attention-getting behavior.

Many books stress the importance of keeping the child in a straight, upright position for swallowing. But children with swallowing disorders may find turning their head to one side and tilting their chin upwards helps to guide liquids away from the airway.

Drinking from a Cup

Drinking from a glass or cup is often difficult for a disabled child to handle. You may have to start with pudding or custard that has been thinned with milk, or milk thickened with unflavored gelatin. If he refuses to let you bring the cup or glass to his mouth, you can start by spooning from the cup. As he tolerates this, increase the number of spoonfuls given in rapid succession, gradually bringing the cup closer to his lips. Eventually you will be close enough to touch his lips with the cup. Next, try alternating sips from the cup with spoonfuls. Always be careful not to let your child drink too rapidly, as he may choke.

If you cut a large semicircle (one to two inches deep) out of one side of a plastic cup, you can pour it into his mouth from the other side without his nose getting in the way. This way you can see the child's lips and the amount he is drinking. Also it will be easier for him as he doesn't have to tip his head as far back.

Appropriate Foods

Thickened purées are easiest to swallow. Try thickening vegetable purées with instant mashed potato flakes or puréed fruits with instant infant cereal (use "Pablum," for example). "Quick Thick" is a commercial thickening product available through the Specialty Food Shop (see page 179).

That store and some other hospitals also sell "Cuisine du Monde," a new line of easy-to-swallow, mousse-type meats and vegetables from Maple Leaf. They can be cut into shapes resembling normal food and picked up with a fork, but require very little chewing.

When ready to move on, start with minced rather than chopped foods. The change-over may need to be very gradual, with just a little minced food added to a purée. Lumps must be very soft. Often instant mashed potato is accepted better than freshly cooked mashed potato.

To improve flavor, add puréed leftover stew or gravies to minced meats.

Foods to Avoid

Asparagus stalks and celery, even if cooked, may still be too fibrous for your child. The skin on peas and creamed corn can cause choking. Many raw fruits and vegetables cannot be chewed sufficiently to be safely swallowed.

Some disabled children have chronic chest problems. For

them, milk may cause mucous that inhibits swallowing. Yogurt, cottage cheese and other cheeses may be better tolerated as the protein has been denatured.

Behavior Modification

Often disabled children are not eating a diet that is varied enough to be nutritionally balanced.

It's tempting to feed the easiest-to-eat foods to the child long after more solid foods could be introduced. This can happen if parents feel sorry for their child because of her disability, or it may be just a matter of failing to notice that the child is finally ready for the next learning stage. As a result, learning to swallow lumps or to chew is delayed in some children. Others become spoiled; they refuse foods they could handle.

Psychologists at the John F. Kennedy Institute in Maryland have developed a successful training program for treating chronic food refusal in disabled children. Here is one example published in the *Journal of Applied Behaviour Analysis*, (Fall 1984).

At sixteen months Joan refused to eat fruits, vegetables, or meats. She did seem to like dry cereal and graham crackers, but her diet was mostly milk. She cried during meals and would even vomit.

To train Joan to eat a more varied diet, a therapist started by working with just two specific training foods — applesauce and puréed carrots. At first, bites of one of the training foods were offered simultaneously with bites of one of Joan's preferred foods — either dry cereal or graham crackers. Gradually a transition was made. A bite of preferred food was given two to three seconds after Joan ate a bite of the training food. Gradually the therapist decreased the frequency of giving the preferred food and required more bites of the training food be eaten first. Praise was also given as positive reinforcement when Joan ate several bites of the training food.

By giving a preferred food soon after Joan accepted a training food, the therapist reduced the likelihood that the training food would be expelled.

Although food expulsion and disruptive behaviors were ignored throughout the training, Joan's crying and interrupting decreased noticeably during treatment. Soon she was readily accepting many fruits and vegetables in her diet.

It's important that behavior training take place, one food at a time, and that adequate nutrition be assured throughout. In Joan's case, she had free access to her favorite foods at supper and six ounces of milk were given between meals. Also she was given a vitamin-mineral supplement until her diet improved. If the child is underweight, sometimes feeding through a temporary gastrostomy is necessary to ensure adequate calories during training phases.

Tray-time-out is a good way to deal with inappropriate mealtime behavior. If the child is disruptive or negative, just move the tray away from the child and turn your back for thirty seconds. Then resume feeding without comment.

If the child deliberately spills food, he should be given a cloth in a firm, but not punitive way and expected to clean up the food. The important training skill is to avoid rewarding unsuitable behavior with undue attention, while rewarding acceptable behavior with your friendly praise and company.

Appropriate Weight

Disabled children are easier to manage if their weight is kept on the low side. But that doesn't mean they should be allowed to become so thin they lack energy to cope with their disability. Growth or puberty should not be delayed.

Standard height and weight charts are not suitable for children who lack muscle tone. Instead, the doctor can use skinfold measurements to determine the amount of lean and fat tissue.

Many books indicate that cerebral palsy children with uncontrolled spastic muscles have very high calorie requirements. However that isn't so. Rather, large amounts of food often need to be offered because as much as two-thirds of the meal ends up on the bib or the floor. Food records are not an accurate way to assess the actual food intake of a disabled child. As a result, cerebral palsy children are often underweight and underfed.

If underweight, you can concentrate foods and add more protein by:

- adding powdered milk to whole milk, mashed potatoes, casseroles, soups, sauces, puddings, eggnogs and milkshakes;
- adding Polycose to beverages and putting brown sugar on cereals;
- adding extra eggs to puddings, casseroles, mashed potatoes;
- offering Sustacal pudding instead of puréed fruit for dessert;
- replacing plain milk with eggnogs, instant breakfast, or commercial supplements such as Ensure, Sustagen, etc.;
- putting extra butter, margarine, cream cheese or peanut butter on bread and crackers.

High-Calorie Fruit Nog

1	egg	1
2 tsp	Sustagen powder	10 mL
½ cup	fruit juice	125 mL

Mix the ingredients together in a blender.
Yield: one ½-cup (125 mL) serving.

192   *Special Feeding Needs of Disabled Children*

The Overweight Child

Some disabled children have very low-calorie needs because they are confined to a wheelchair or otherwise not active. If these children are allowed to become too fat, it will detract from their appearance and social acceptance. As well, their disability will be harder to manage.

But low-calorie needs do not mean low fluid requirements. Food and beverages will need to be diluted.

To reduce calories use:

- skim milk rather than two percent or homo milk;
- lean meats that have been broiled, baked or stewed rather than fried;
- fresh fruit and fruit juices as snacks instead of candy or sweetened pop (Diet pop is acceptable as a calorie-free beverage);
- herbs and spices for seasoning, rather than rich cream sauces, gravy or mayonnaise.

When Constipation Is a Problem

Constipation is a chronic problem with disabled children, either because of lack of intestinal muscle tone or because they are dehydrated. All too often they are just given more bran, and that compounds the problem. Although adequate fiber is essential, adding bran to the diet only makes the problem worse if adequate fluid isn't provided.

Think about the number of times you sip coffee, water, juice or other beverages throughout the day. It's not as easy for the disabled child who can't reach for a glass or handle a cup. Even when water is close at hand, he is dependent upon someone thinking to give it to him. For some children each mouthful carries the risk of aspiration, so they avoid drinking as often as possible.

Thickening fluids can reduce the embarrassment of drooling, but if the thickening agent increases the solute load on the kidney, fluid requirements only become greater.

Too often, even doctors fail to diagnose dehydration. All it takes is a simple urine test. A urine test that is at the upper normal level for concentration should not be ignored. The child may have no fluid reserves. He will run a fever as soon as the weather turns hot.

The Child with a Severe Swallowing Disorder

- Choking
- Drowning
- Death
- Humiliation

were words some disabled teens used when Dr. Lance Levy asked them to describe the experience of being fed.

A pediatrician at the Hospital for Sick Children who specializes in treating swallowing and feeding disorders, Dr. Levy sees many malnourished and dehydrated children of all ages. For these children the fear of gagging or choking often overrides the desire to eat or drink.

Parents and caregivers may spend hours feeding a child what seems to be inordinately large amounts of food, but the child may still be malnourished.

When a disabled child is not adequately nourished, his muscles weaken; his condition degenerates; he loses his desire to struggle with his disability; and he may become listless or irritable. Growth will be stunted; puberty delayed.

All children, including the disabled, have a right to adequate nutrition and to be given an opportunity to eat or be fed with dignity. Dr. Levy believes that when more than an hour is needed to feed a child one inadequate meal, it's time to consider alternatives such as gastrostomy as a temporary or permanent solution.

Gastrostomy involves feeding through a tube which goes directly through the abdomen into the stomach. Dr. Levy has seen remarkable improvement within twenty-four hours of initiating supplementary feedings via this route. The child feels instantly better. His behavior improves.

"Children with gastrostomies can still eat some food, but the meal time needn't occupy a disproportionate amount of time," says Levy. "Now there is time to do other things. And the gastrostomy doesn't interfere with activities, including sports such as soccer or swimming."

When finally given a gastrostomy after several years of unsuccessful feeding, older children say it's the first time they ever remember not being hungry or thirsty.

Medications and Foods

Many medications used in the treatment of chronic conditions interact with the nutrients in foods. Therefore they must be given between meals.

Others are better tolerated if taken with meals. Therefore, when you have your child's prescription filled, ask your pharmacist or doctor when the medication should be given and follow her instructions carefully.

Some medications cause drowsiness, nausea or alter taste. Discuss this with your doctor or a dietitian. These professionals may be able to give you some practical suggestions for overcoming these side effects.

Feeding your disabled child may be difficult, but it is of paramount importance. If you are not having success, demand more help. It's there, but not always easy to obtain.

15

NUTRITIONAL BALANCE

Sensible eating involves selecting a mix of foods throughout the day that will provide all the necessary nutrients needed for body growth, maintenance and health. Canada's Food Guide to Healthy Eating makes that easy by dividing foods into four groups — grain products, vegetables and fruit, milk products, and meat and alternatives. The Food Guide then recommends a range of servings from each food group for anyone over the age of four. If you follow Canada's Food Guide when planning your family's menus, it's very likely that everyone will be achieving balanced nutrition.

When dietitians talk about balanced nutrition, they are referring to the need to obtain the right amount of each nutrient — protein, fat, carbohydrate, vitamins and minerals — in relationship to body needs. And needs change as children grow.

Although children need differing amounts of each nutrient, it doesn't mean that the nutrients needed in greater quantities are more important than the others. Indeed, the action of nutrients is interrelated. For example, certain B vitamins play an essential role in converting starch and sugar to energy. When your child needs more energy for growth or activity, she needs more of these B vitamins. Another example of an interrelationship is calcium and vitamin D. Calcium in foods can't be absorbed unless the body also has sufficient vitamin D. There are many more examples.

Energy Balance

We measure food energy in calories (and sometimes the metric equivalent, joules). Without enough calories, children fail to grow; too many calories and they become fat. Calories, or energy, come from four sources — proteins, fats, carbohydrates and alcohol. (Since this book is about children, we can leave out discussion of the calories in alcohol.)

Fat is the most concentrated source of energy, with more than twice as many calories per unit weight as carbohydrate (which includes both sugar and starch) and protein: fat has nine calories per gram, while the other two have only four calories per gram.

Balanced nutrition for children includes all three sources of energy, or calories.

Because fat is a concentrated source of calories, it packs a lot of energy in a small volume. That's ideal for the small baby. Indeed, over fifty percent of the energy in breast-milk is in the form of fat. But later, as the child grows, his stomach can handle more food and meals can be less dense. Then, thirty percent of calories from fat is more appropriate. That's why we advise you to cut back on fatty and fried foods.

Carbohydrate calories come in two general forms — sugars, which are quickly absorbed and used for energy, and starches, which are more slowly absorbed. Very young babies need sugar — the sugar in milk. In the first couple of months their digestive systems are not ready to break down starches. But as they become older, the more slowly absorbed starches are appropriate as a regulated source of energy. This is the reason I've urged you to emphasize cereals and vegetables as important sources of carbohydrate for older infants and toddlers.

Protein plays a dual role, as the building material for muscles and body cells, and as a source of energy. Nutritional balance means providing enough protein each day for cell growth and replacement, but not excessive amounts. That's because the extra protein isn't stored; it's broken down and one of the by-products, urea, must be excreted through the kidney. Too much urea excretion can put a strain on an immature kidney.

Vitamin and Mineral Balance

Similarly, vitamin and mineral intakes need to be balanced with the child's needs and energy intake. One vitamin isn't more important than another; sometimes increasing the intake of one vitamin even increases the need for another.

The chart on page 200 summarizes the function and common food sources of many of the vitamins and minerals. You can see that most nutrients are in a variety of foods, so that if you give your child foods from Canada's Food Guide, he will be getting the essential nutrients.

Nutrients are needed in small amounts. Larger amounts are not better and can even be dangerous. The chances of overdosing on one vitamin, relative to another, are rare if foods are the sources of vitamins. Your child would have to eat an unrealistic amount of one type of food to overdose on a vitamin. Not so, with supplements. It's unfortunately very easy to give an overdose, and some supplement overdoses can make your baby very sick. They can even kill.

That's why I don't believe in giving multi-vitamin/mineral pills as "just in case" insurance. Most of the time it's a waste of money, and it can be risky having these pills around. At those times when a supplement is appropriate (see page 38), follow the dosage instructions carefully. Don't overdose. And treat vitamin-mineral supplements the way you would all medications. Keep them well away from curious children.

Vitamins and Minerals:
Their Uses and Sources

Nutrient	*Function*	*Food Sources*
Vitamin A	• healthy skin and mucous membranes • bone and tooth development • night vision • reproduction	• dark green and bright yellow fruits and vegetables: carrots, cantaloupe, broccoli, squash, sweet potatoes, apricots, watermelon and peaches
Vitamin B1 (thiamin)	• used in deriving energy from sugar and starches • normal growth • appetite	• pork, beef, liver, whole grain and enriched breads and cereals, rice, green vegetables, legumes and peanuts
Vitamin B2 (riboflavin)	• maintenance of healthy skin, eyes, nails and hair • normal growth	• milk and dairy products, organ meats, leafy vegetables, peanuts, fish, eggs, enriched breads and cereals
Vitamin B3 (niacin)	• energy production • fat stores • nerve action • formation of hormones • healthy skin	• legumes, organ meats, fish, eggs, peanuts, dried fruits, whole grain and enriched breads and cereals

Nutrient	Function	Food Sources
Vitamin C	• healthy gums • wound healing • iron absorption • formation of hormones • protein metabolism	• citrus fruits and juices, strawberries, cantaloupe, green peppers, tomatoes, potatoes, leafy green vegetables; added to fruit juices and fruit drinks
Vitamin D	• absorption of calcium • growth of soft tissues	• sardines, herring, salmon, tuna, eggs, liver; added to all milk and infant formulas
Calcium	• bones and teeth • nerve impulses • regulates heart beat • cell wall structure	• milk and milk products, sardines, salmon, broccoli, walnuts
Iron	• carries oxygen in blood • transports oxygen to muscle cells	• organ meats, red meats, dried fruits, egg yolks, nuts, spinach; whole grain and enriched breads, cereals and pasta products

There are other essential vitamins and minerals; folic acid, vitamin B12, vitamin E, iodine, magnesium and zinc. However these nutrients are contained in the same foods as the key vitamin and minerals above. Therefore, if you plan your child's diet to incorporate foods from Canada's Food Guide, there is a good chance you will be providing all the essential vitamins and minerals.

Balance in Foods

The balance concept can also be applied to foods. Eggs provide many essential nutrients, but we've all heard about the danger of too much cholesterol from too many eggs. Similarly, milk is an important source of protein, calcium and several vitamins — but some children drink too much milk. They don't have room left for enough of the other important foods, particularly the foods high in iron.

That's why I don't like "good" or "bad" labels for foods. Too often, the so-called "bad" foods take on a special significance; we think of them as the better-tasting foods. Nutrition becomes mixed up with value judgments. Besides, even a food rich in fat or sugar, such as a piece of cake, isn't always inappropriate if balanced with other foods that day which contain plenty of the other essential nutrients.

However, meals can be out of balance if several high-fat foods are served. That's why, throughout this book, I've pointed out the high-fat or sugar-rich foods. These are the foods in which the proportion of other nutrients, relative to fat and sugar, is small.

Fiber

Fiber is another nutrient frequently mentioned throughout this book. Fiber is the part of food that gives it its structure and shape. Broccoli, wheat bran, potato skins all contain fiber. Humans can't digest fiber; it passes through their intestinal tract absorbing water and providing substance for muscle action.

The amount of fiber you give your baby must also be balanced — too much and she'll have diarrhea; too little and she'll be constipated. That's why I've cautioned against bran cereals for toddlers, and why instead I recommend whole grain breads and cereals.

Check with a Professional Dietitian

Offering balanced nutrition is like every other aspect of parenting. It requires a background of knowledge and a little common sense. If, after reading this book, you have specific questions about your child's eating habits, seek the advice of a qualified professional dietitian. To find one, call your local hospital or health unit, or provincial dietetic association or health ministry. Before your consultation, check the dietitian's qualifications. Is he or she a member of the Canadian Dietetic Association? That's your guarantee that the advice you will be receiving is reliable.

CANADA'S
Food Guide
TO HEALTHY EATING

Health and Welfare
Canada

Santé et Bien-être social
Canada

Enjoy a variety
of foods from each
group every day.

Choose lower-
fat foods
more often.

Grain Products
Choose whole grain
and enriched
products more
often.

Vegetables & Fruit
Choose dark green and
orange vegetables and
orange fruit more often.

Milk Products
Choose lower-fat
milk products more
often.

Meat & Alternatives
Choose leaner meats,
poultry and fish, as well
as dried peas, beans and
lentils more often.

Canada

Different people need different amounts of food, depending upon their age, body size and activity. Canada's Food Guide to Healthy Eating suggests a range that can apply for most people over the age of four.

Grain Products

| 5-12 servings daily | 1 serving:
1 slice bread
or 175 mL (¾ cup) cooked cereal
or 30 g (1 oz) cold cereal | or ½ roll, bun, bagel or muffin
or 125 mL (½ cup) cooked rice, macaroni, spaghetti or noodles |

Vegetables & Fruit

| 5-10 servings daily
Use fresh, frozen or canned produce or juice. | 1 serving:
125 mL (½ cup) vegetables
or 1 medium size potato, carrot or tomato
or 250 mL (1 cup) salad | or 125 mL (½ cup) fruit juice
or 1 medium-sized peach, apple, orange or banana
or 125 mL (½ cup) stewed fruit |

Milk Products

| Children 4-9 years:
2-3 servings
Youth 10-16 years:
3-4 servings
Adults: 2-4 servings
Pregnant and Breast-feeding women:
3-4 servings | 1 serving:
250 mL (1 cup) whole, partly skimmed or skim milk
or 175 g (¾ cup) yogurt | or 50 g (1 oz) regular or low-fat cheese
or 2 slices processed cheese
or 250 mL (1 cup) milk pudding |

Meat & Alternatives

| 2-3 servings daily | 1 serving:
50-100 g (1½-3 oz) cooked lean meat, fish or poultry
or 1-2 eggs | or 125-250 mL (½-1 cup) cooked peas, beans or lentils
or 30 mL (2 tbsp) peanut butter
or 100 g (⅓ cup) tofu |

Other Foods

Taste and enjoyment can also come from other foods and beverages that are not part of the four food groups. Some are higher in fat or calories, so use them in moderation.

RECIPE INDEX

GENERAL INDEX

Alcohol, 16, 24
Allergies, 17, 42, 175-182
  breast-feeding and, 12, 14, 23
  coping with, 178-179
  recipes, 179-182
  symptoms of, 175-177
  tests for, 176-177
Amino acids, 166
Antibodies in breast milk, 17
Appetite, 44, 78
  see also Feeding cues
Areola, 18-19
Art, use of food in, 139, 145

Baby food, 50-61
  commercial, 50-52, 58-60
    storage, 59
    toddler foods, 77
  homemade, 51-58
    preparation, 52-58
    storage, 53-54
Bacon, 124
Behavior modification, 190-191
Beverages, 37-38, 82, 120, 130-131, 143, 192
Bottle-feeding, 8, 12-13, 15-17, 29-37
  advantages and disadvantages, 15-17

  bedtime bottles, 36
  weaning, 29
  see also Formula
Botulism, 65, 124
Bread, 91, 123-124, 153-154
  when breast-feeding, 22
Breakfast, 94-98, 120-124, 144, 151-154
Breast care, 17-19, 28
Breast-feeding, 8, 11-12, 13-31
  advantages and disadvantages, 15-17
  alcohol when, 16, 24
  cleft palate and, 185
  contaminants and, 24-25
  drugs when, 24
  expressing milk, 28
  let-down reflex, 20, 21
  milk supply when, 20-21, 22, 23, 25-26
  mother's diet when, 21-24
  myths about, 14
  smoking when, 24
  solids and, 43
  supplementing with a bottle, 26-27
  weaning, 29
  working and, 29
Butter, 131

210

Menu, 48-49
Microwave
  heating formula in, 36
  preparing baby food in, 53
  reheating foods in, 59-60, 81
  see also most recipes
Milk, 29-32, 82, 90
  as an allergen, 176-177
  breast or formula, 11-13
  chocolate milk, 130
  cow's milk, 62-63
  energy in, 198
  flavored milk, 130-131
  nutrients in, 22-23, 202
  powdered, 131, 192
  supply, 25, 43
  when breast-feeding, 22-23
Minerals, 199, 201
MSG (monosodium glutamate), 50

Niacin, 200
Nipple, 185
  mother's, 18-19
Nitrate and nitrite, 47
Nursery school, 145-147
Nursing, 13-14, 15, 27
  see also Breast-feeding
Nursing bottle syndrome, 36-37
Nutrition, 6, 8, 194
Nuts, 166, 169-170
  as a snack, 150, 151

Oils, *see* Fats
Overfeeding, 13
Overweight
  fat consumption and, 132
  grazing and, 150
  in baby, 66-67
  in disabled child, 193
  in toddler, 100-101

PCB (polychlorinated biphenyl), 25
Phenylketonuria (PKU), 178
Phosphorus, 31
Picnics, 141-142, 143
Polycose, 192
Pop, 131
Pork, 157-159
Potassium, 120
Poultry, 90, 159-161
Protein, 22-24, 29, 30-31, 42, 74, 94-95, 98, 100, 123, 125, 143
  as an allergen, 175
  complete and incomplete, 166-167

Rash, 14, 69
Refusing foods, 70
Restaurants, children in, 142-143
Riboflavin, 200

Safety, 134, 141-142
Salmon, 125
Salt, 50
  see also Sodium
Sensitivities to foods, 14, 177-178
Serving sizes, 78, 79, 89-91
Shellfish, as an allergen, 176
Snacks, 92
  from grandmother, 145
  from neighbors, 144-145
  at daycare, 145-147
  in the car, 149
  see also Grazing
Sodium, 50
  in commercial baby foods, 50
  in cured meats, 124
  in fast foods, 143
  in frozen dinners, 128